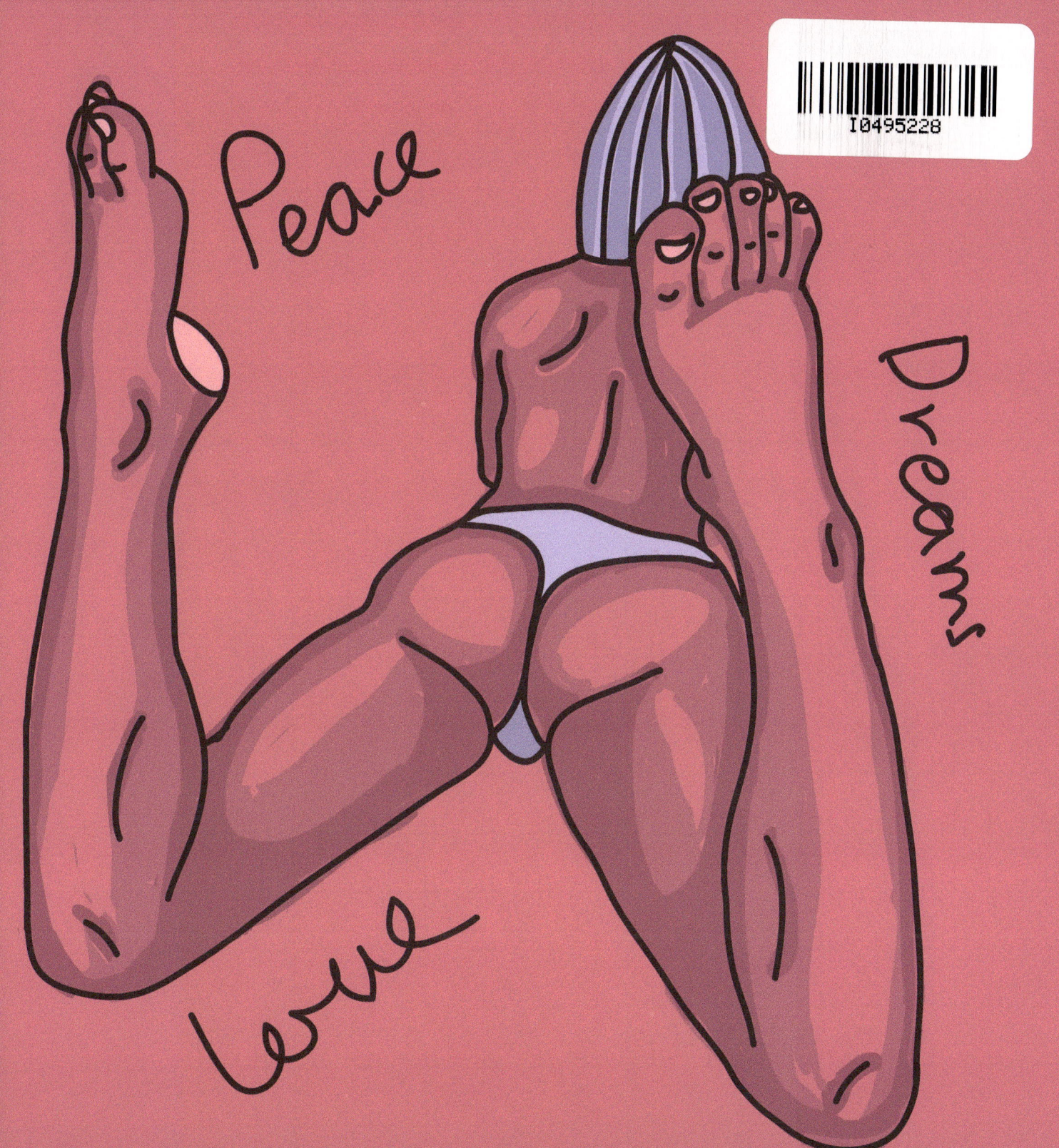

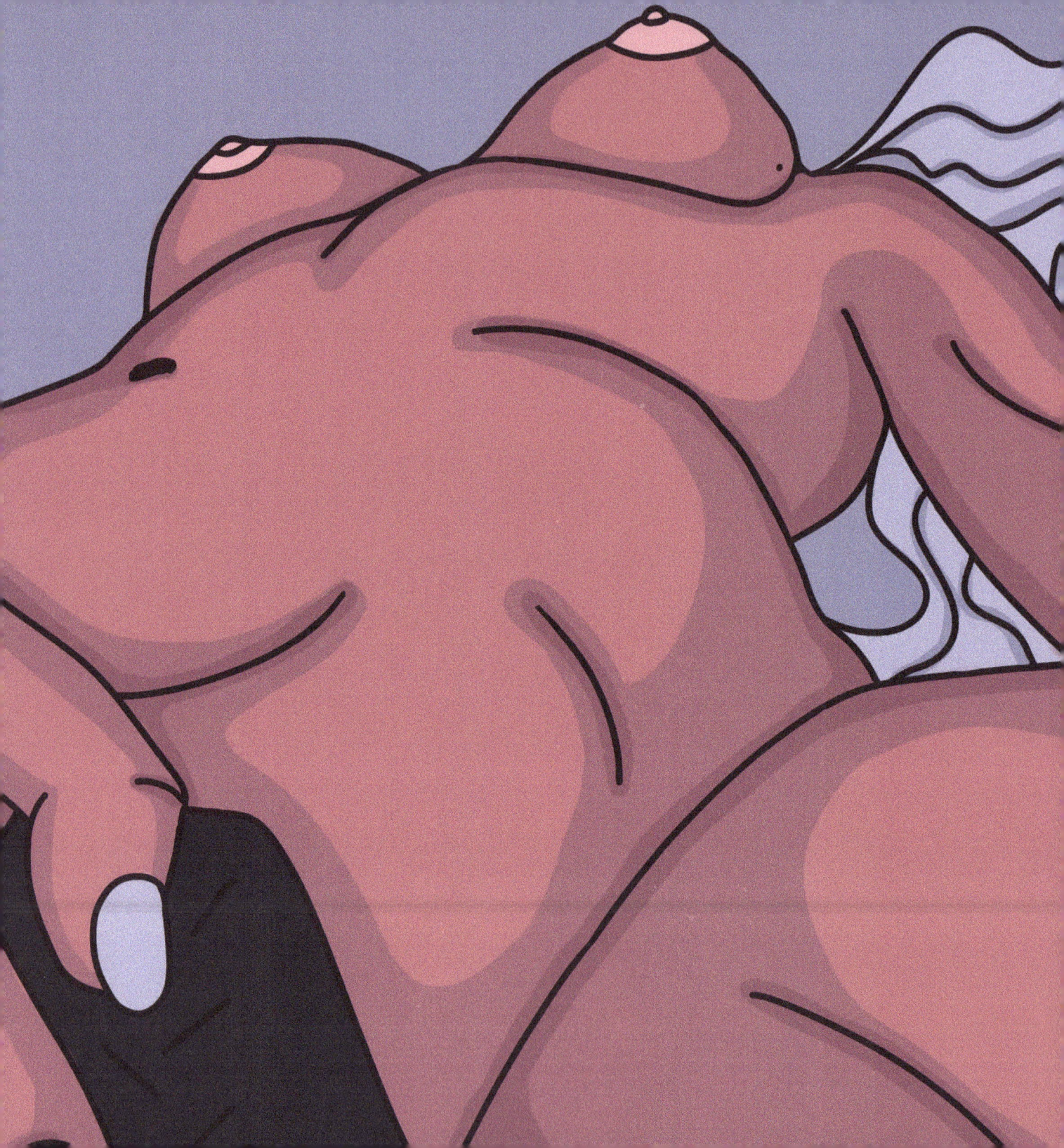

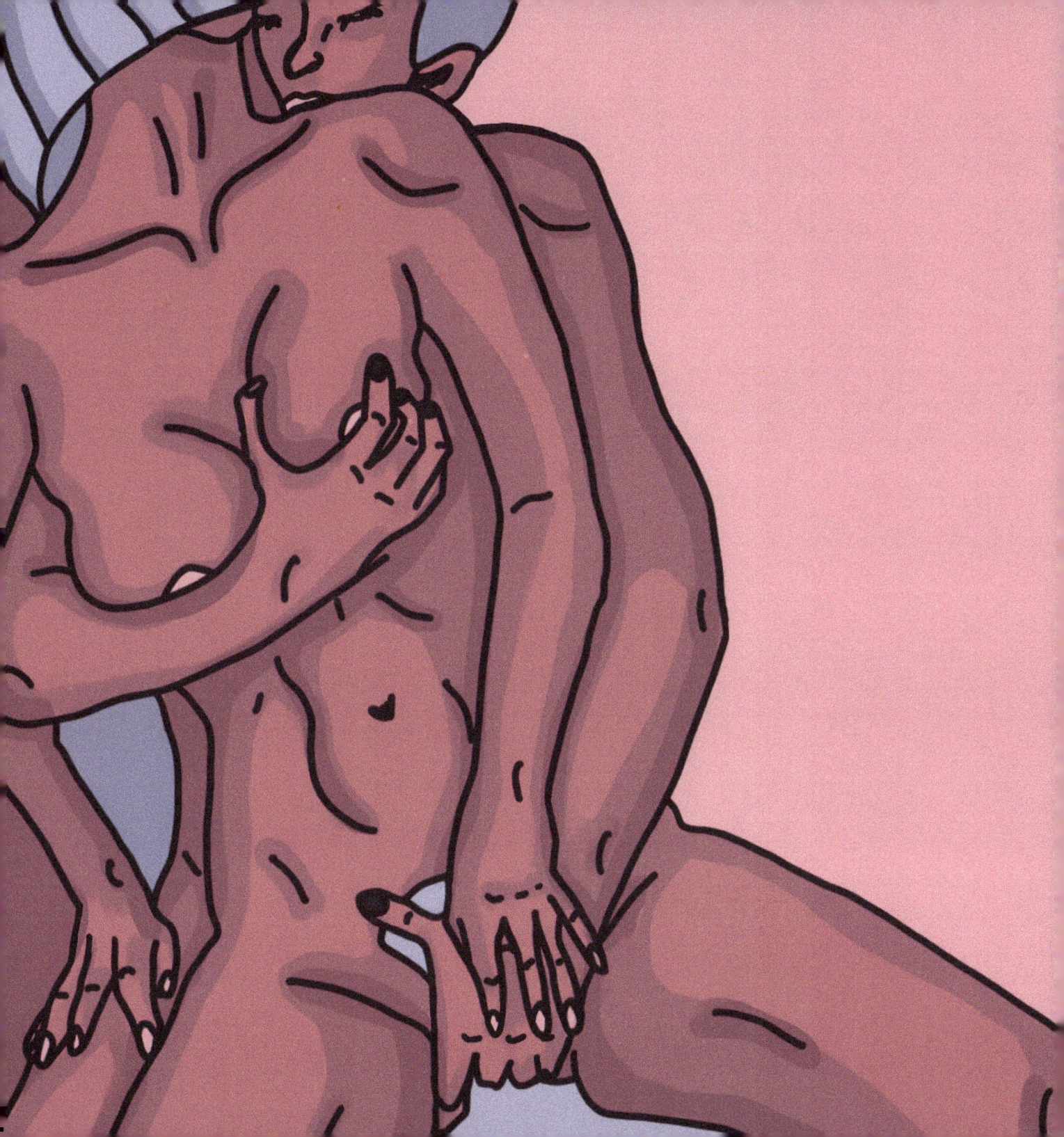

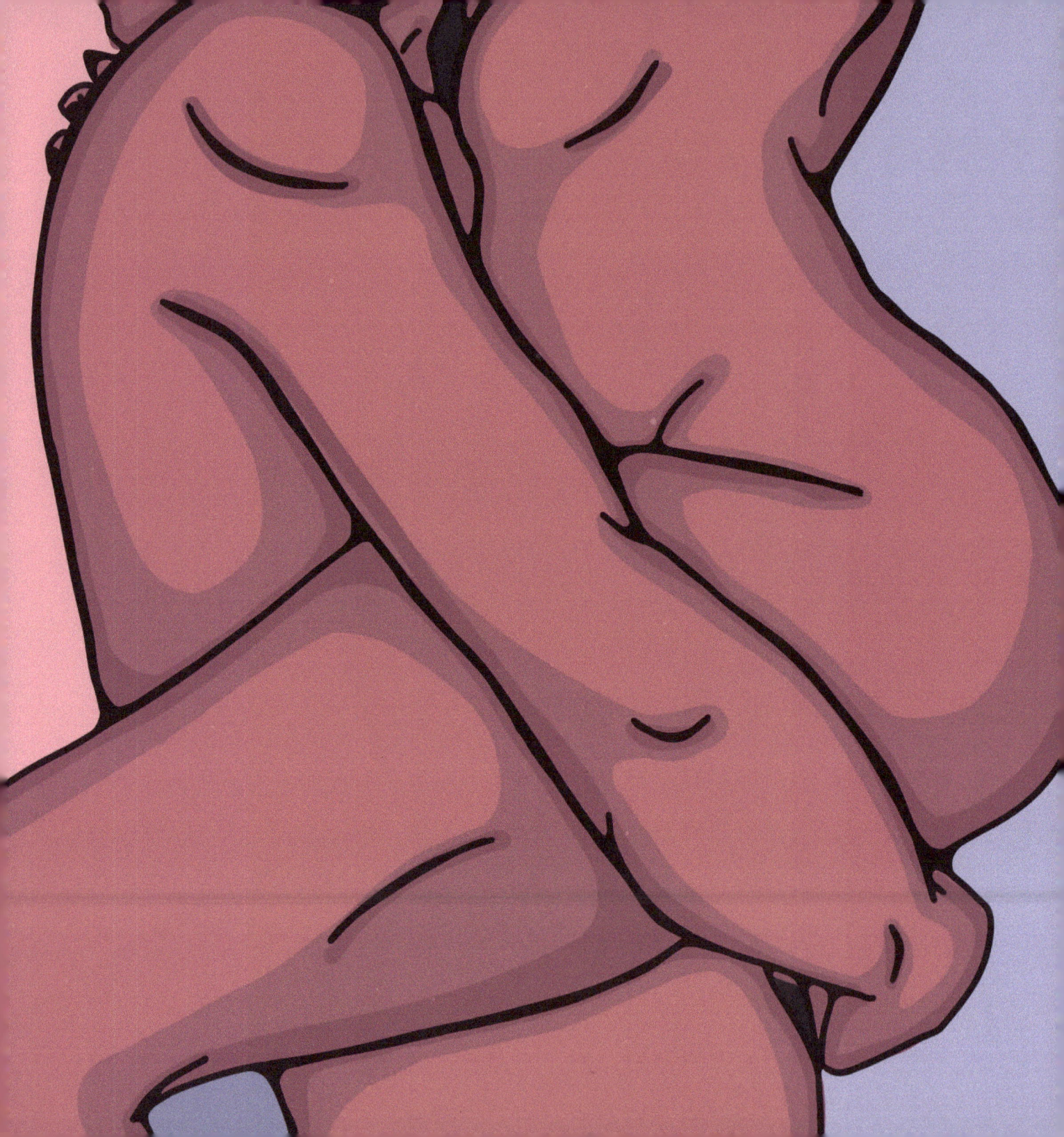

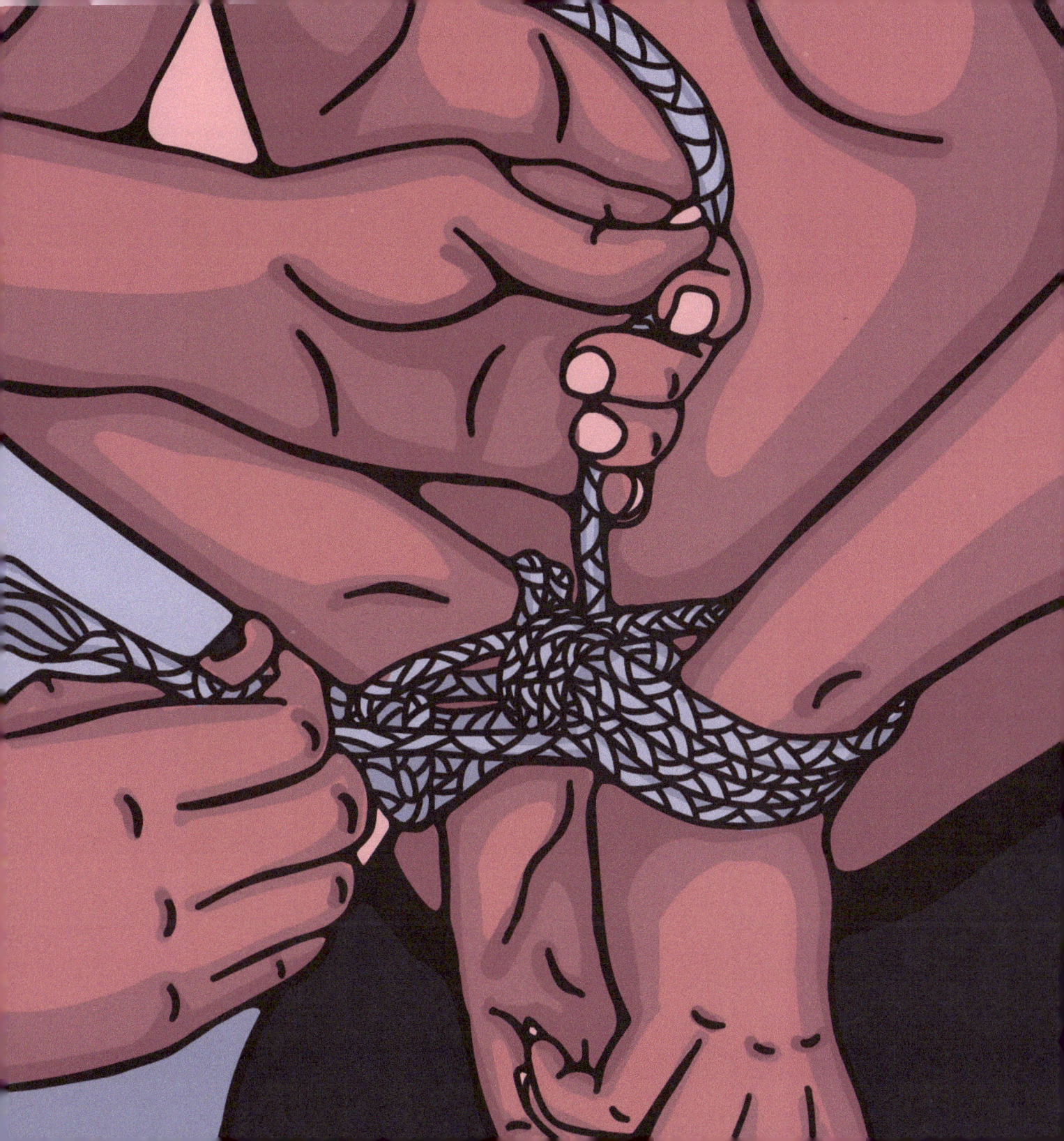

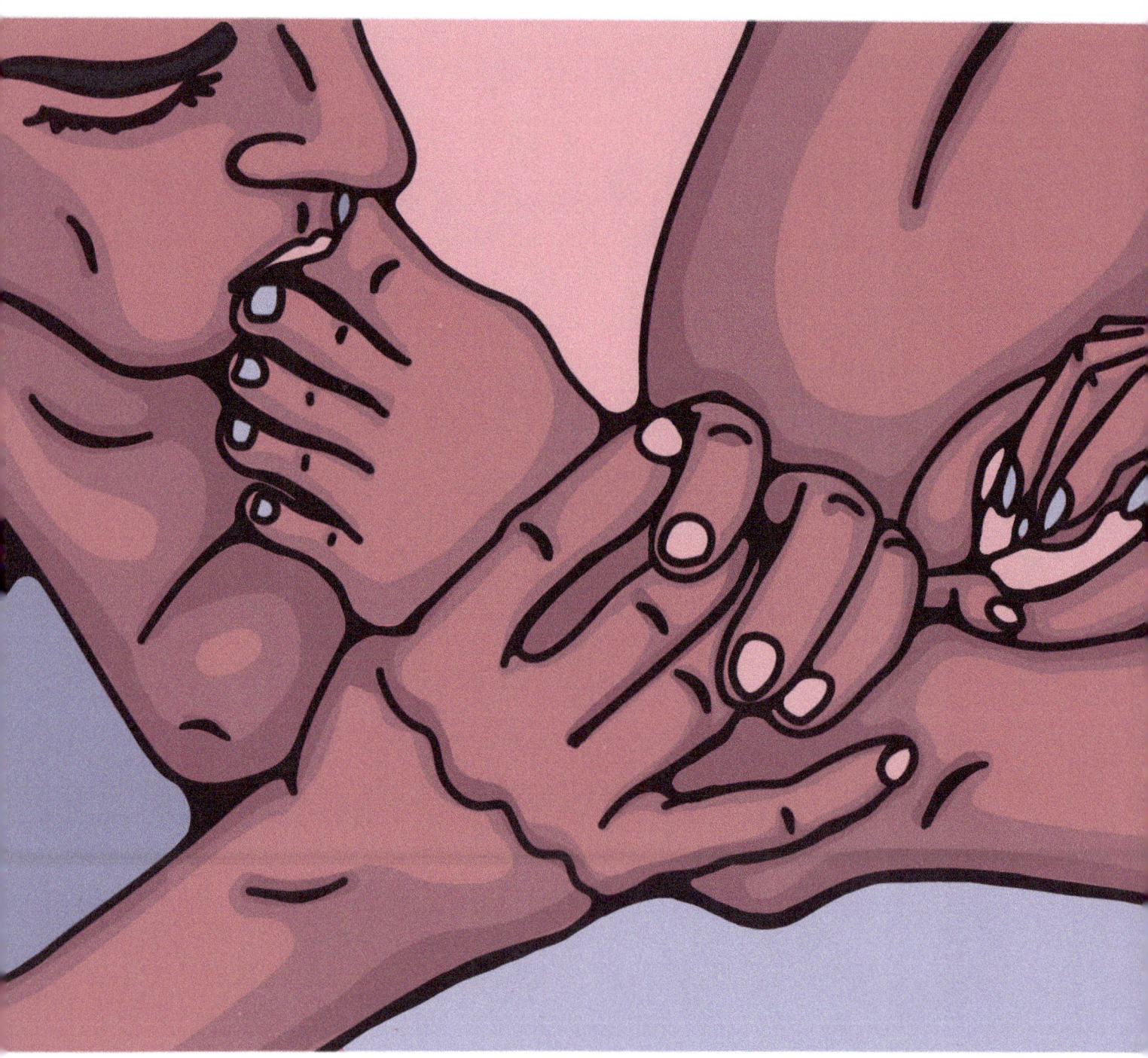

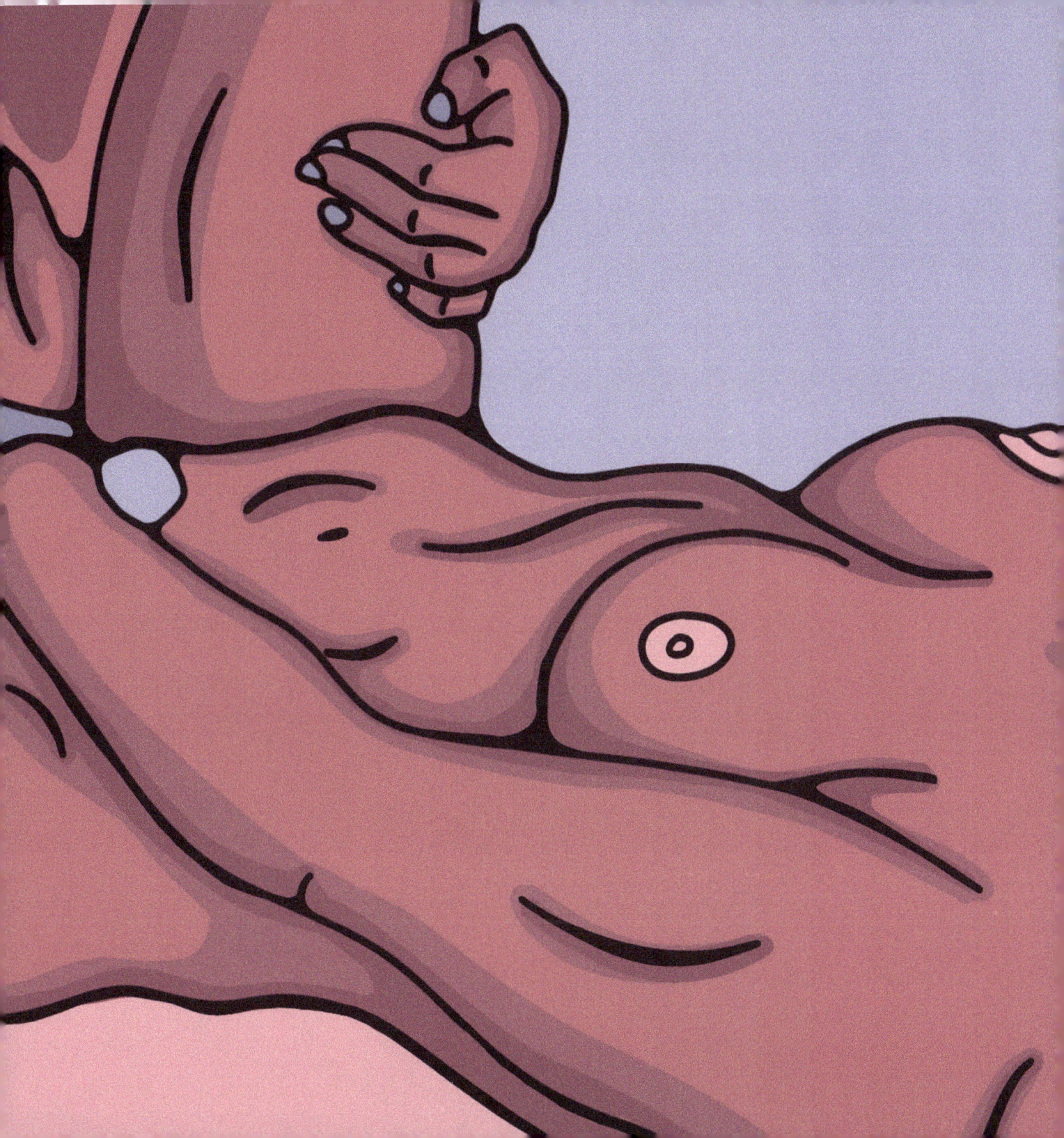

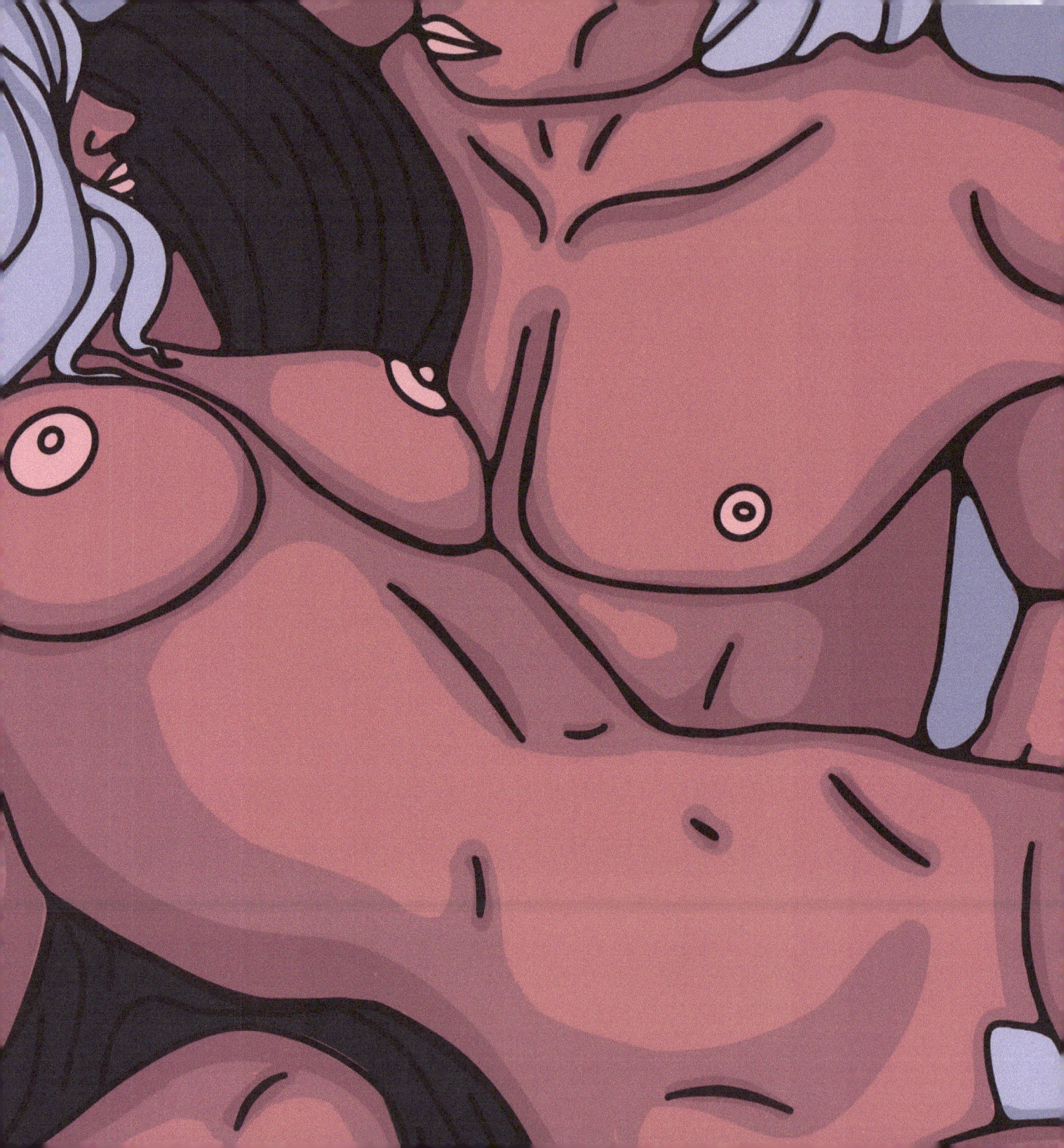

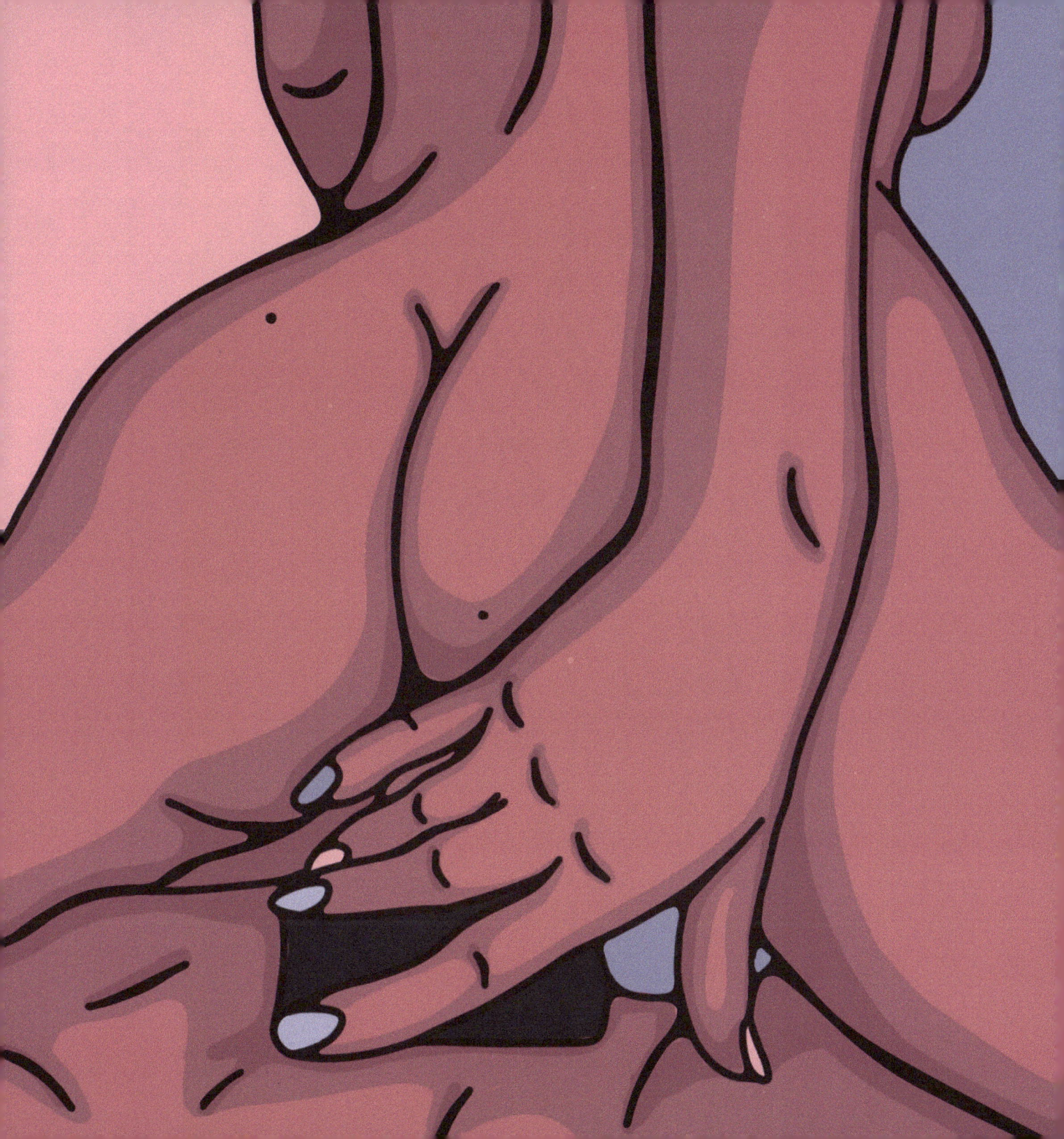

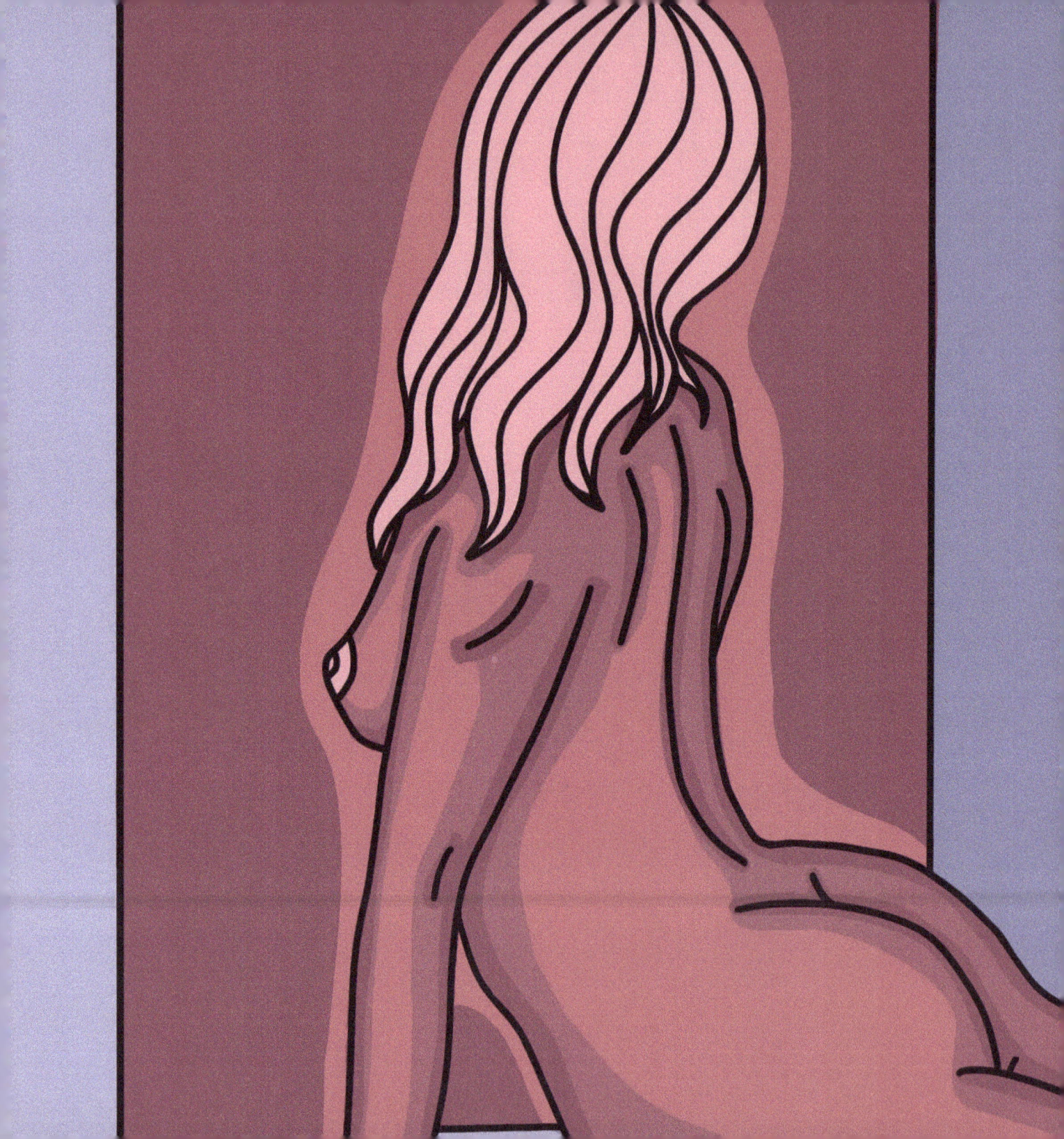

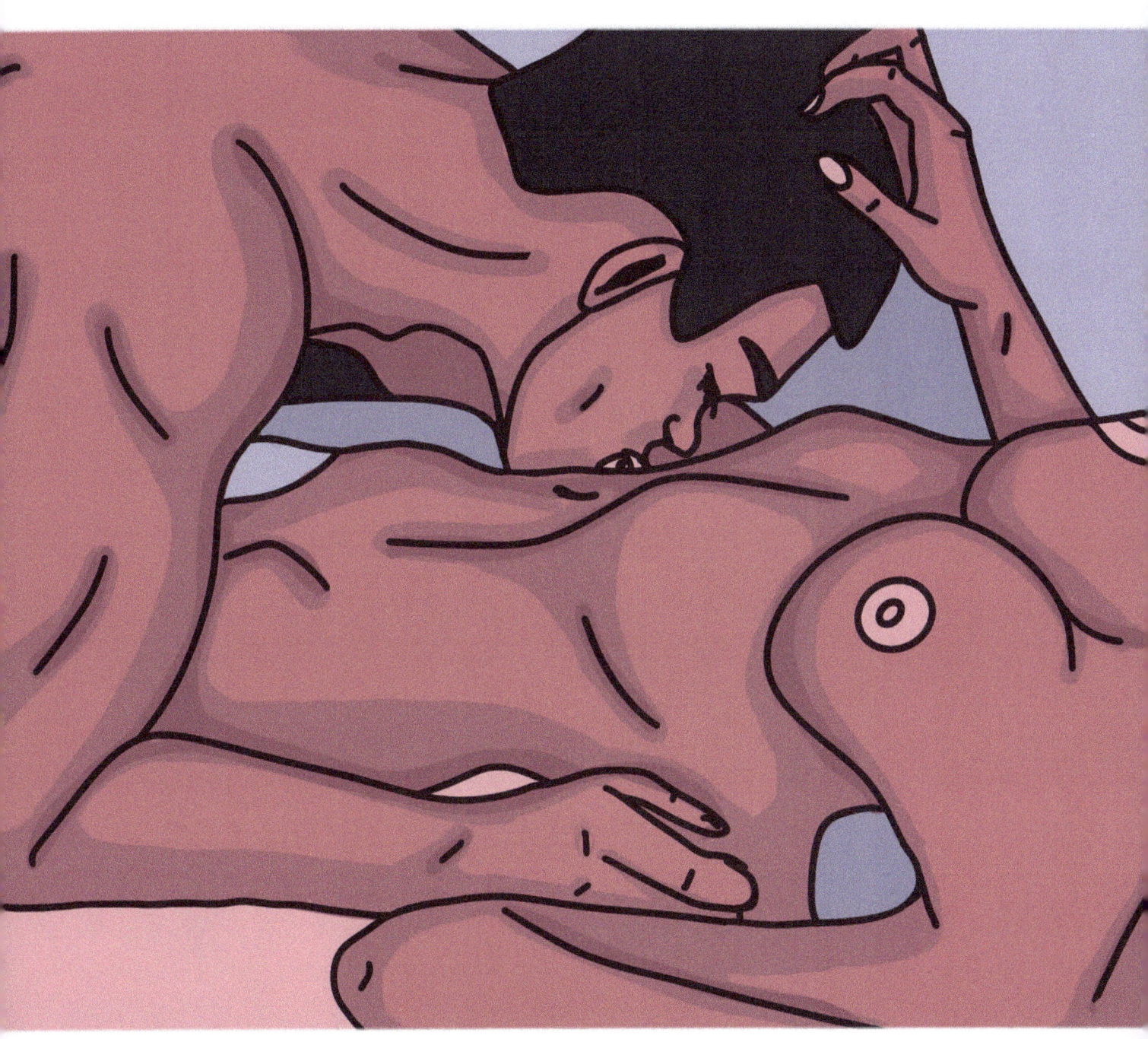

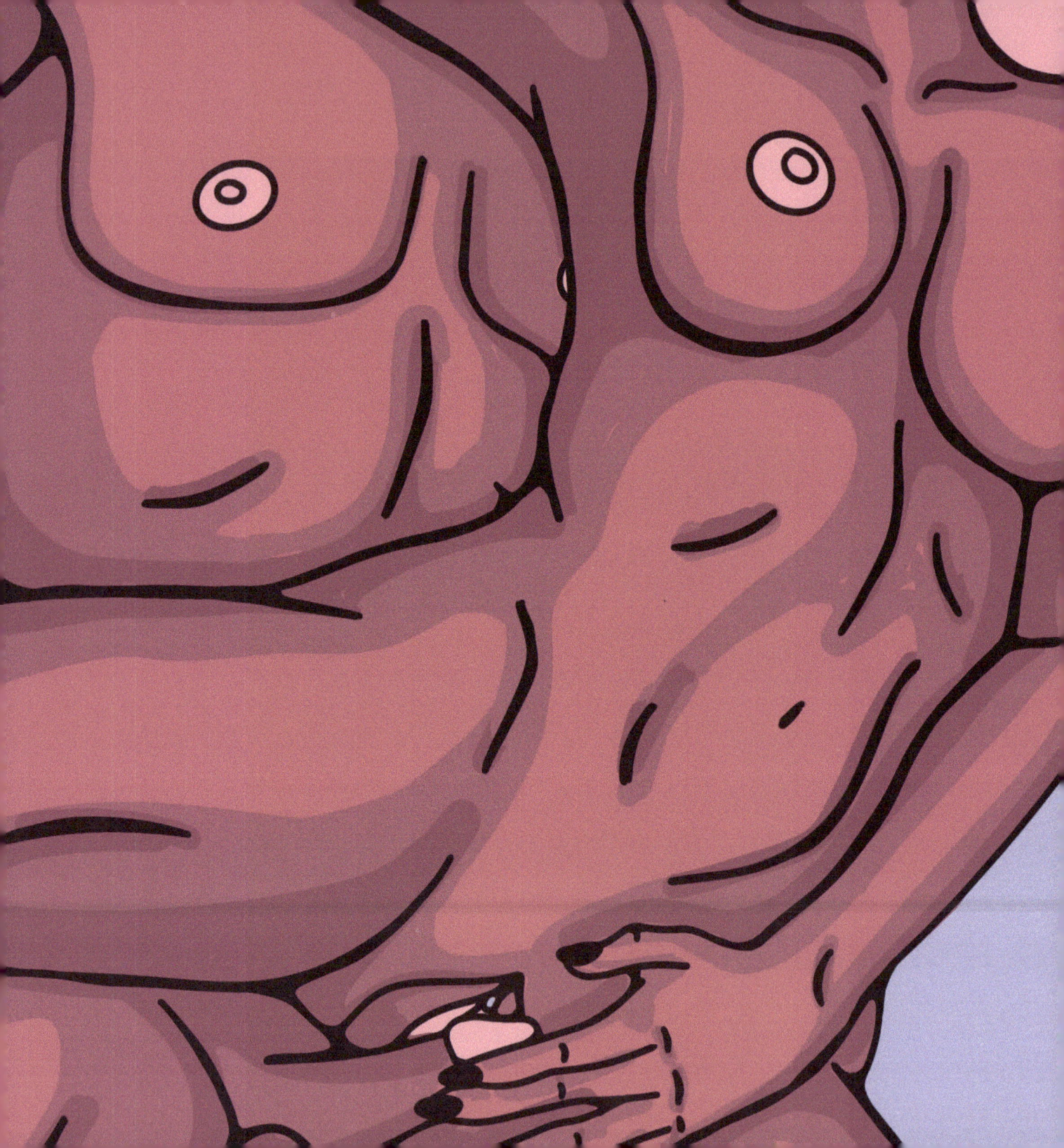

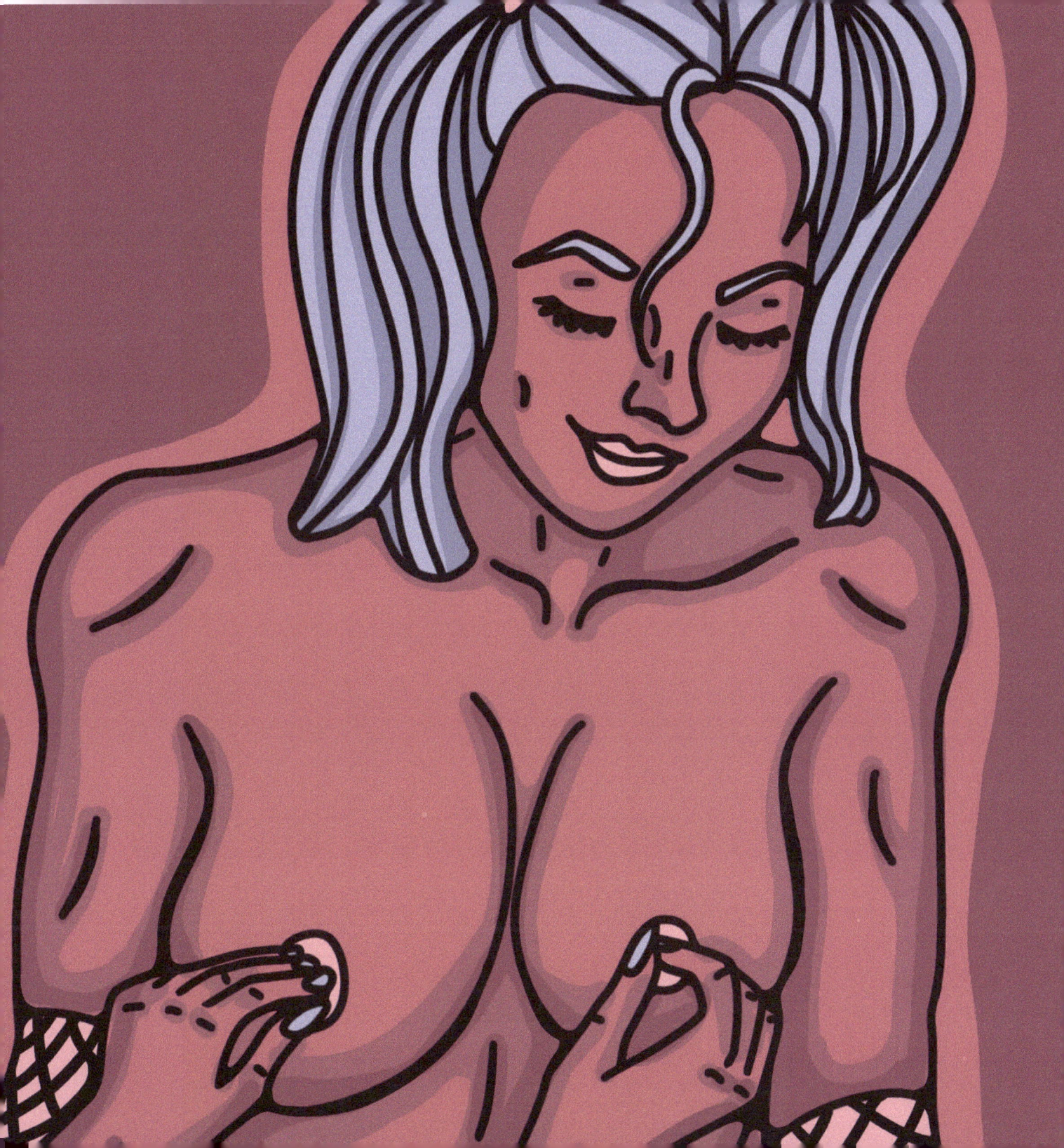

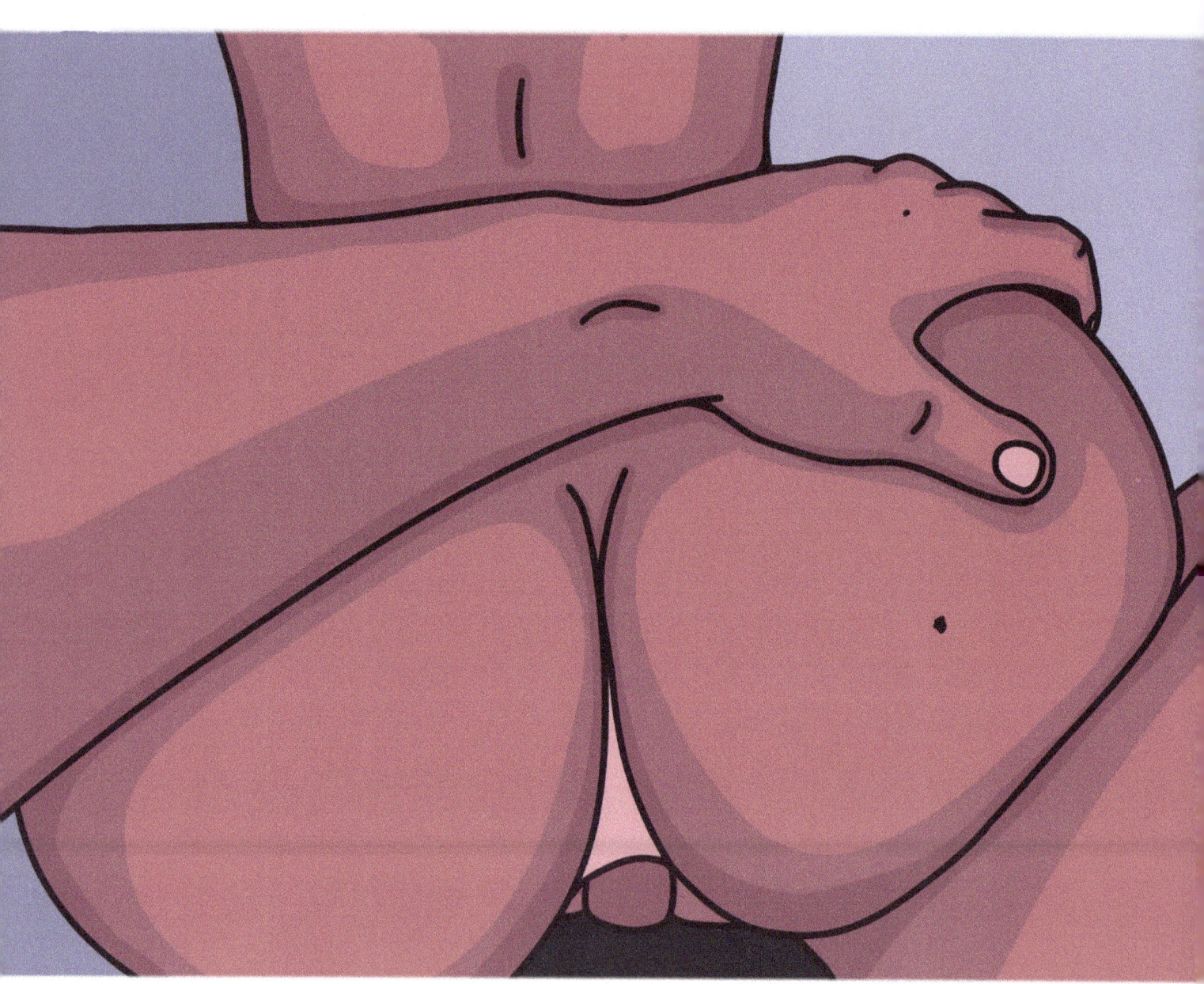

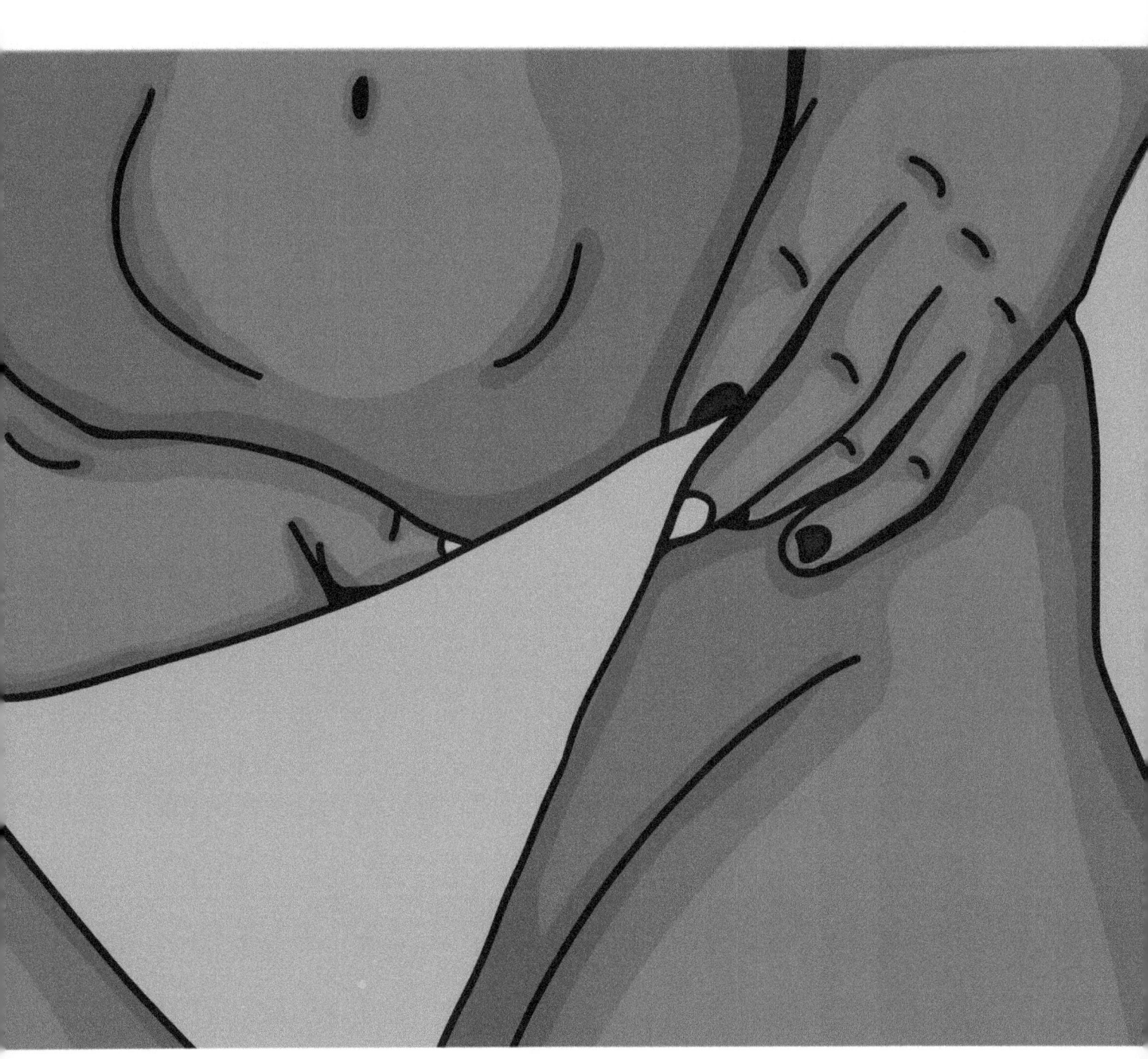

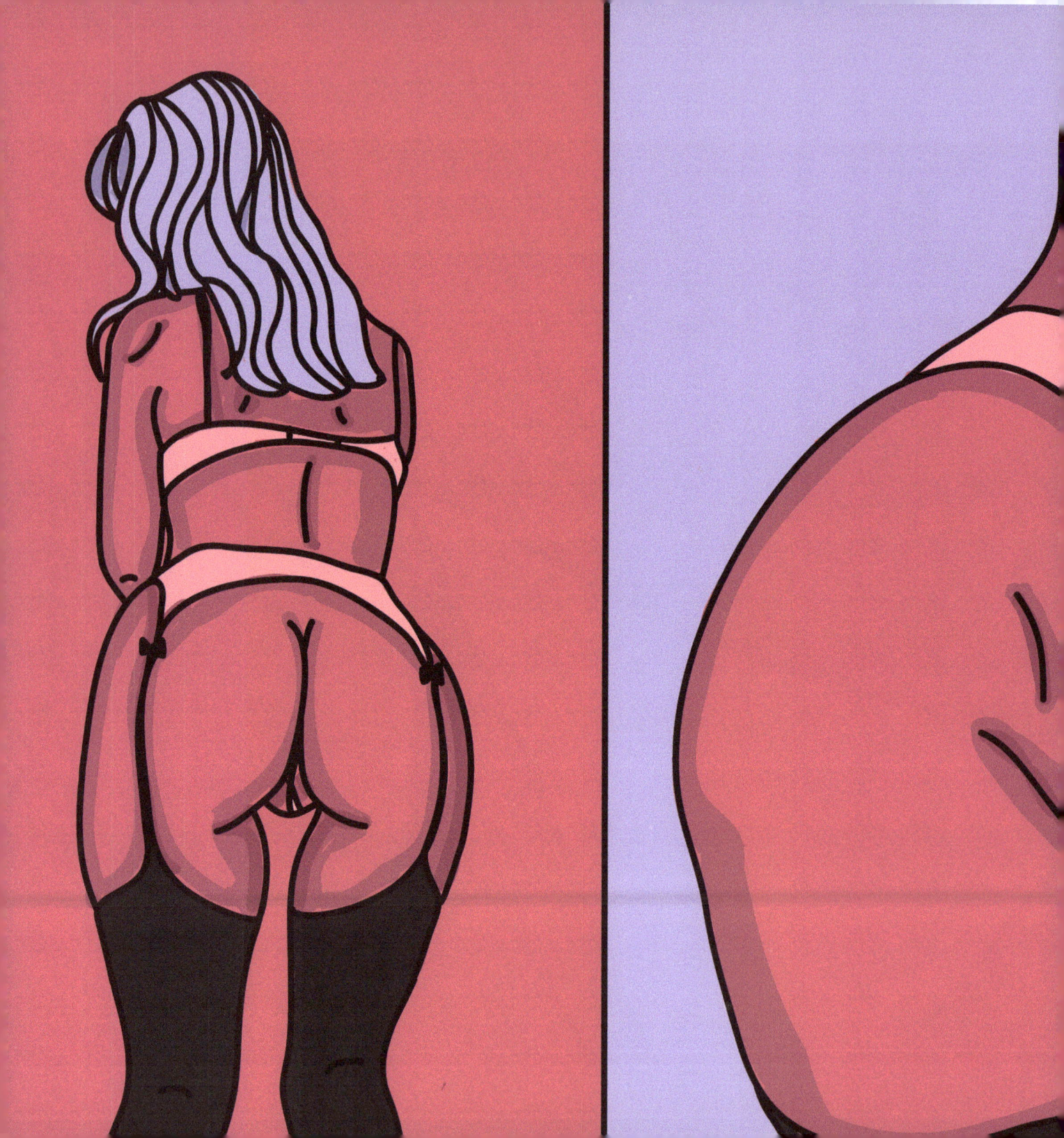

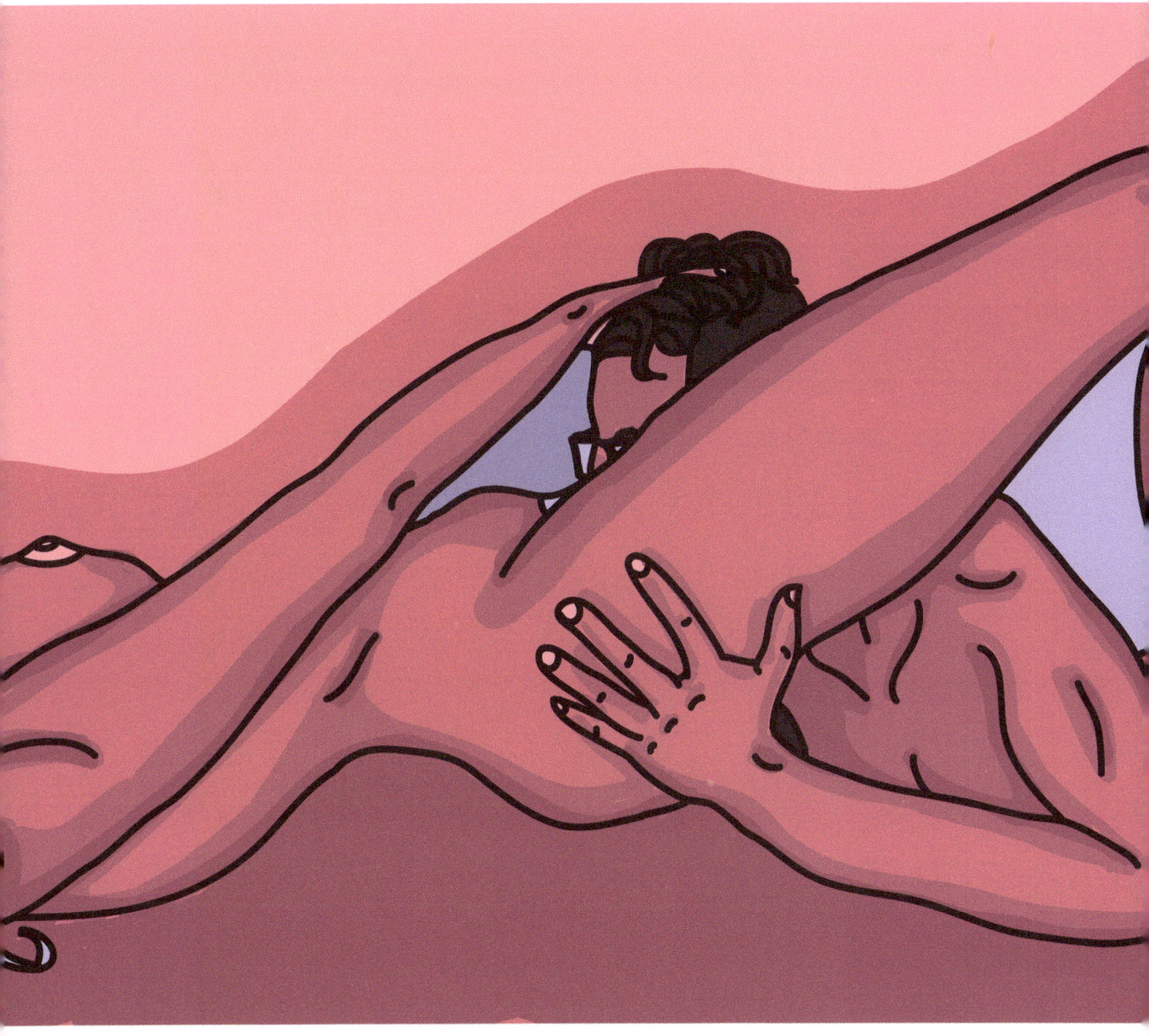

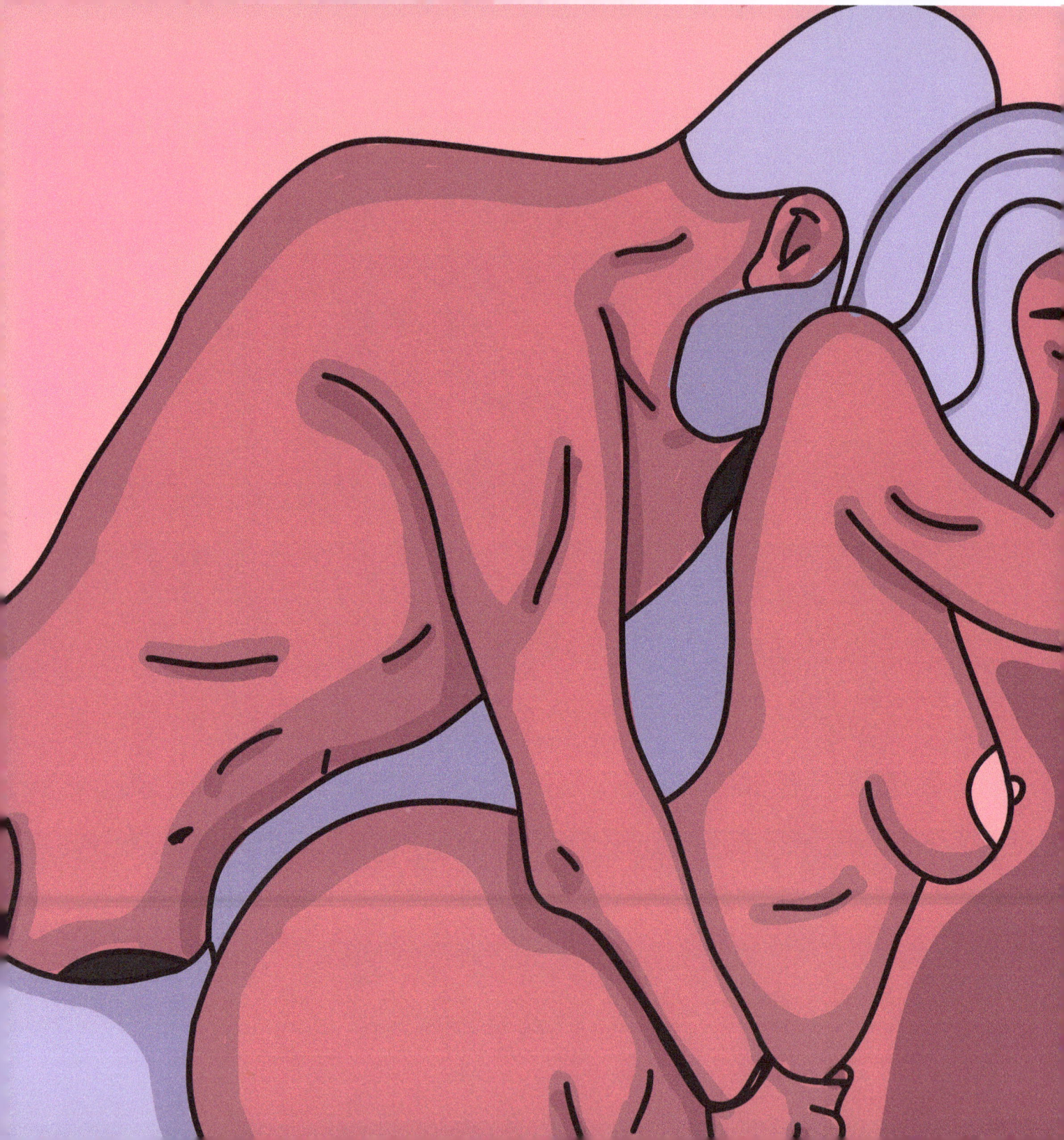

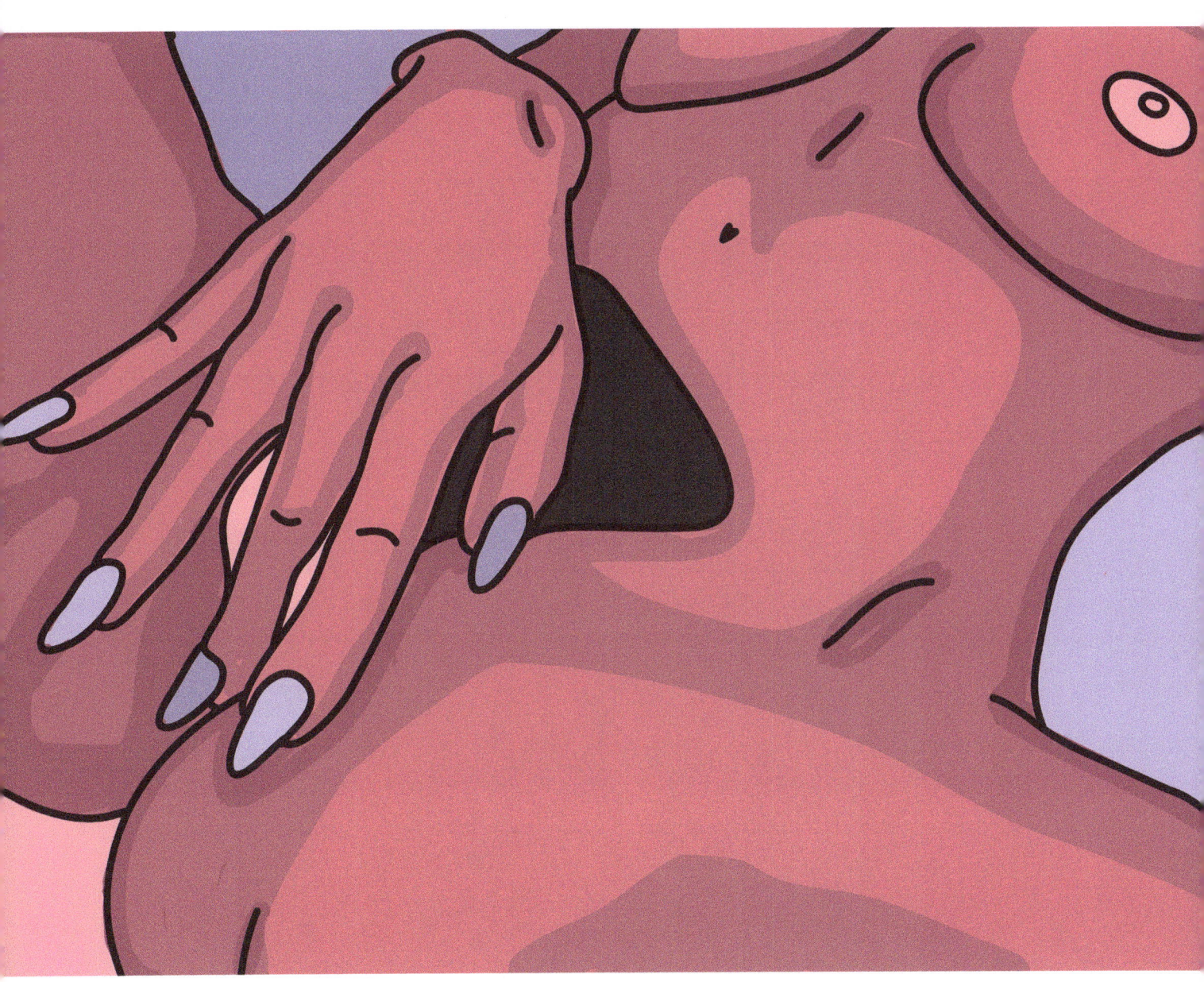

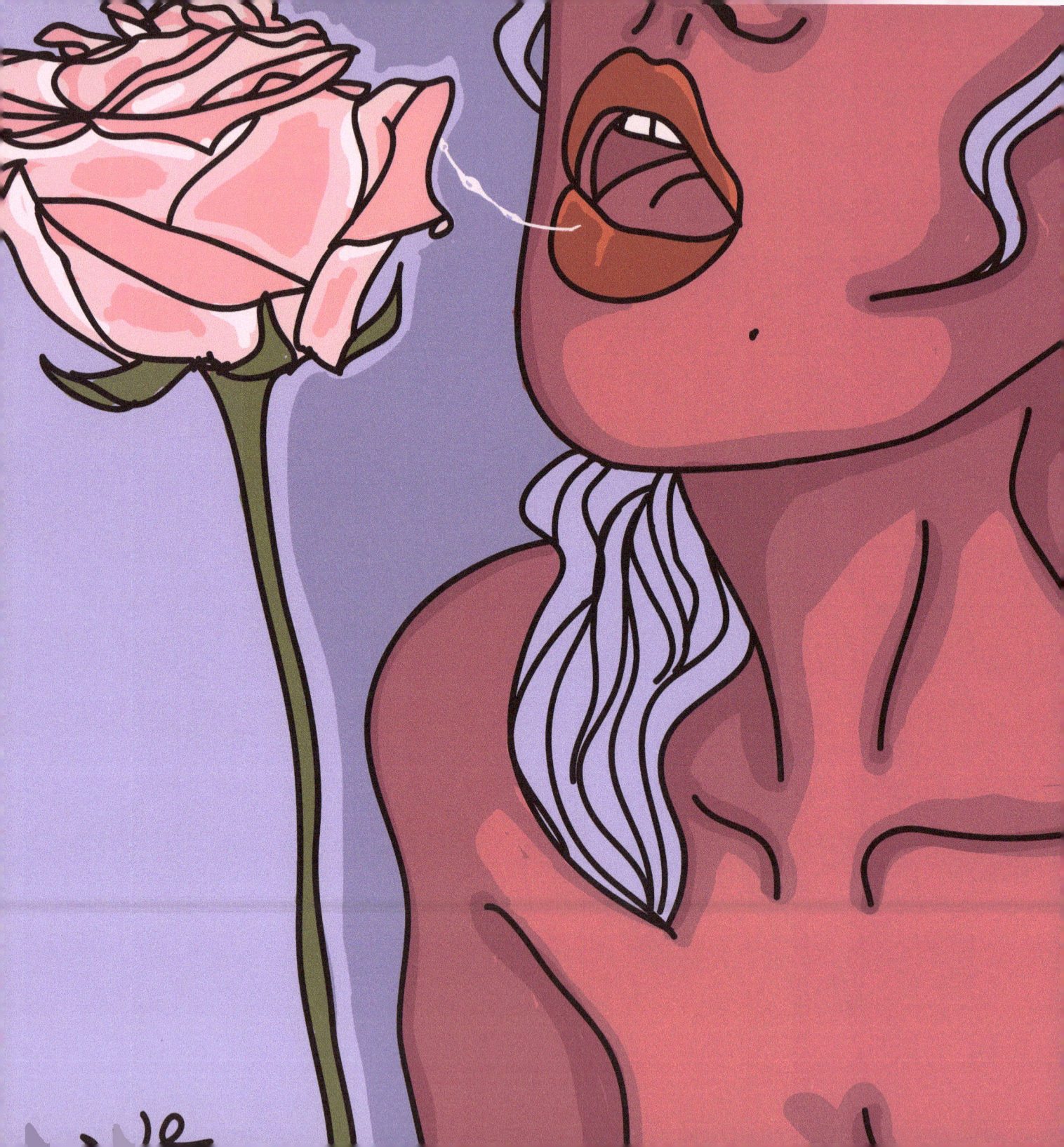

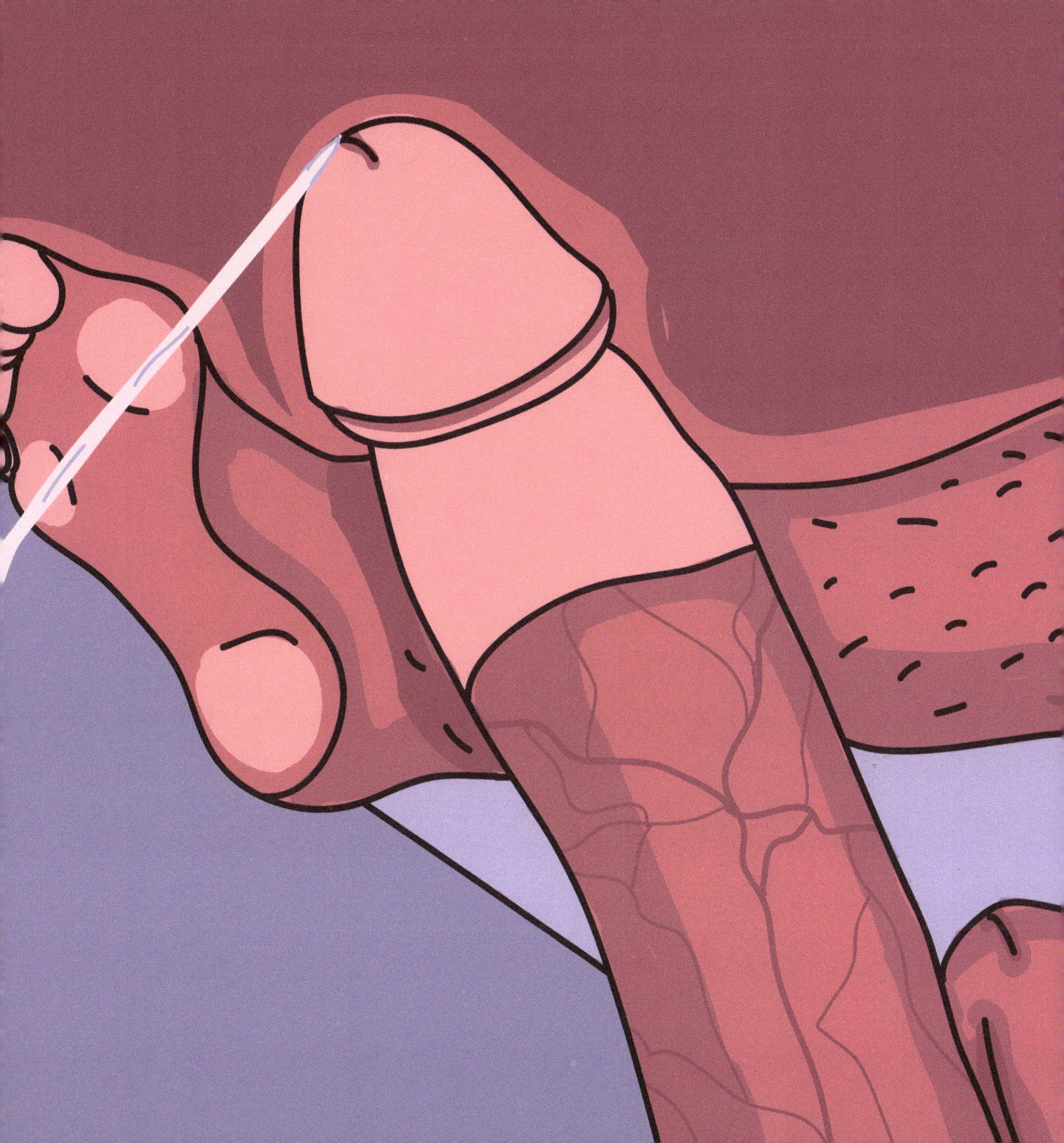

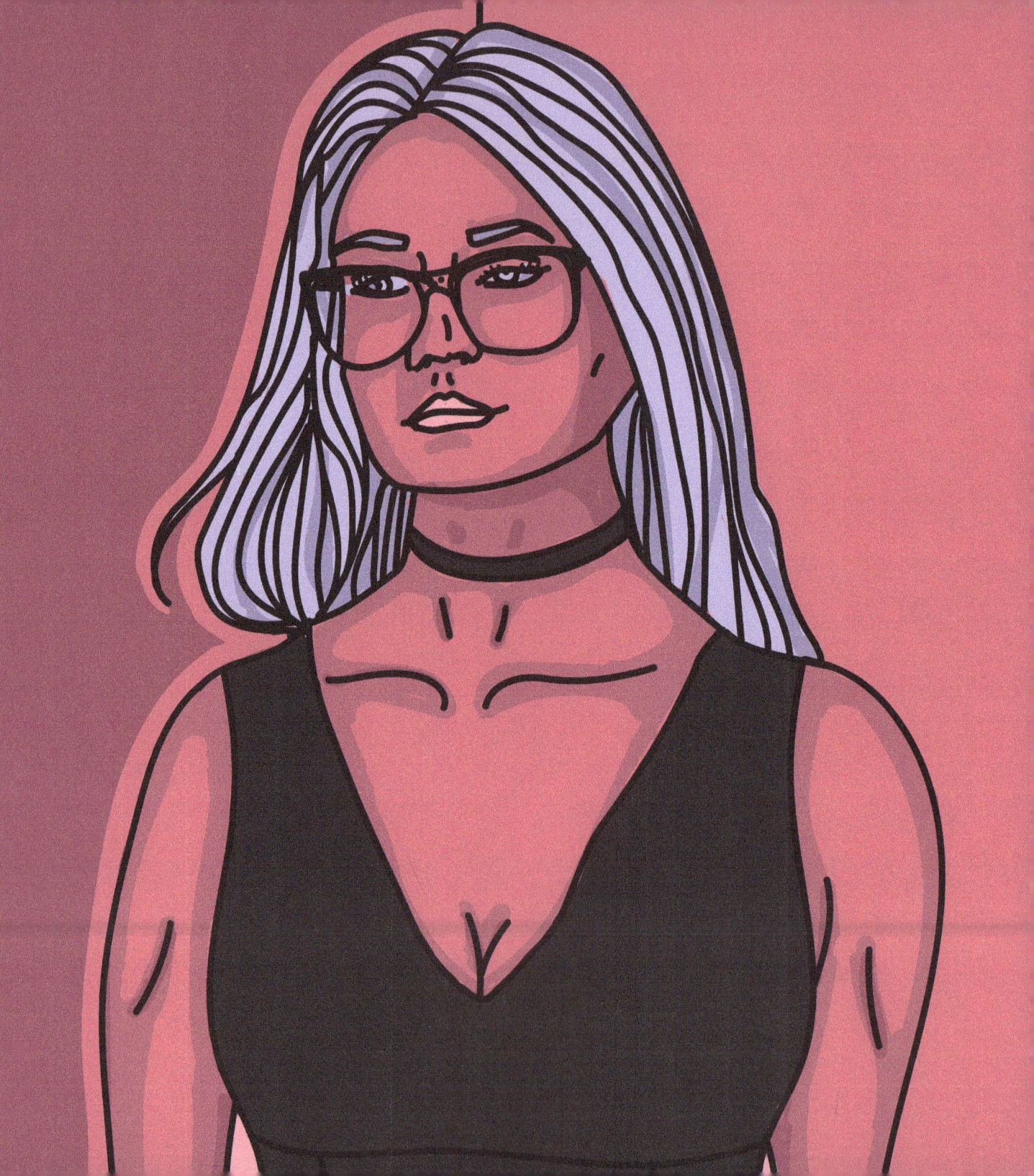

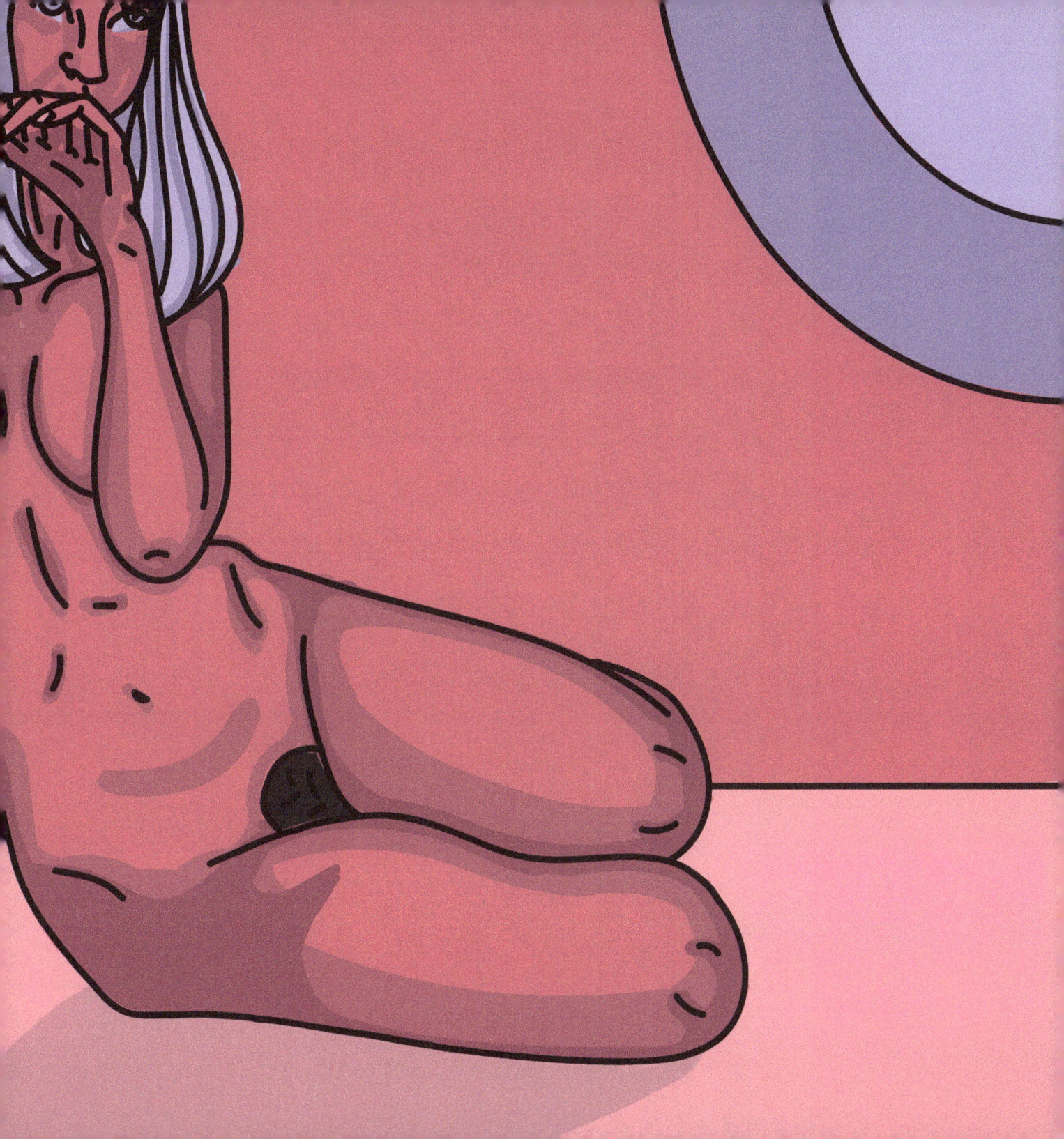

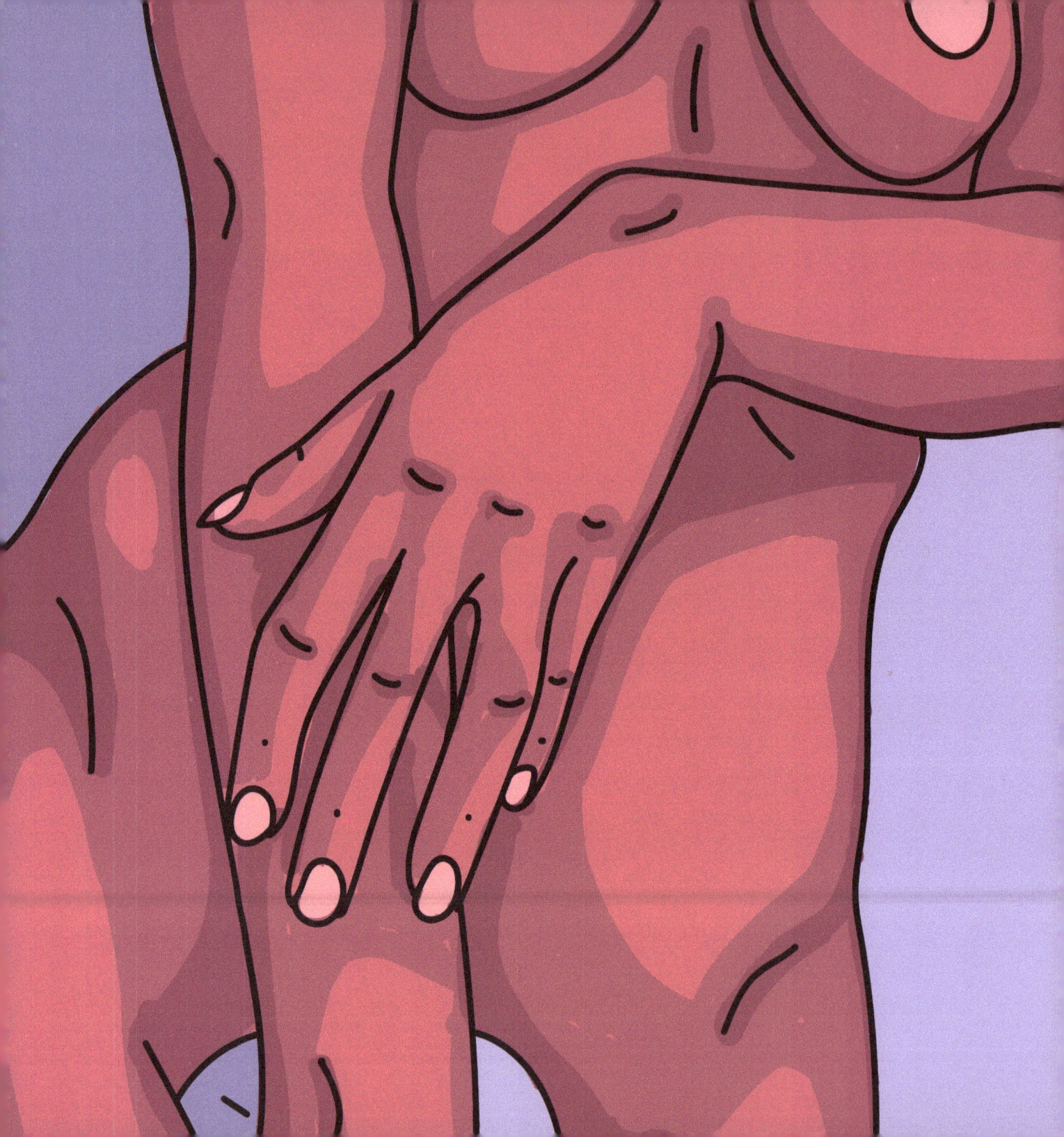

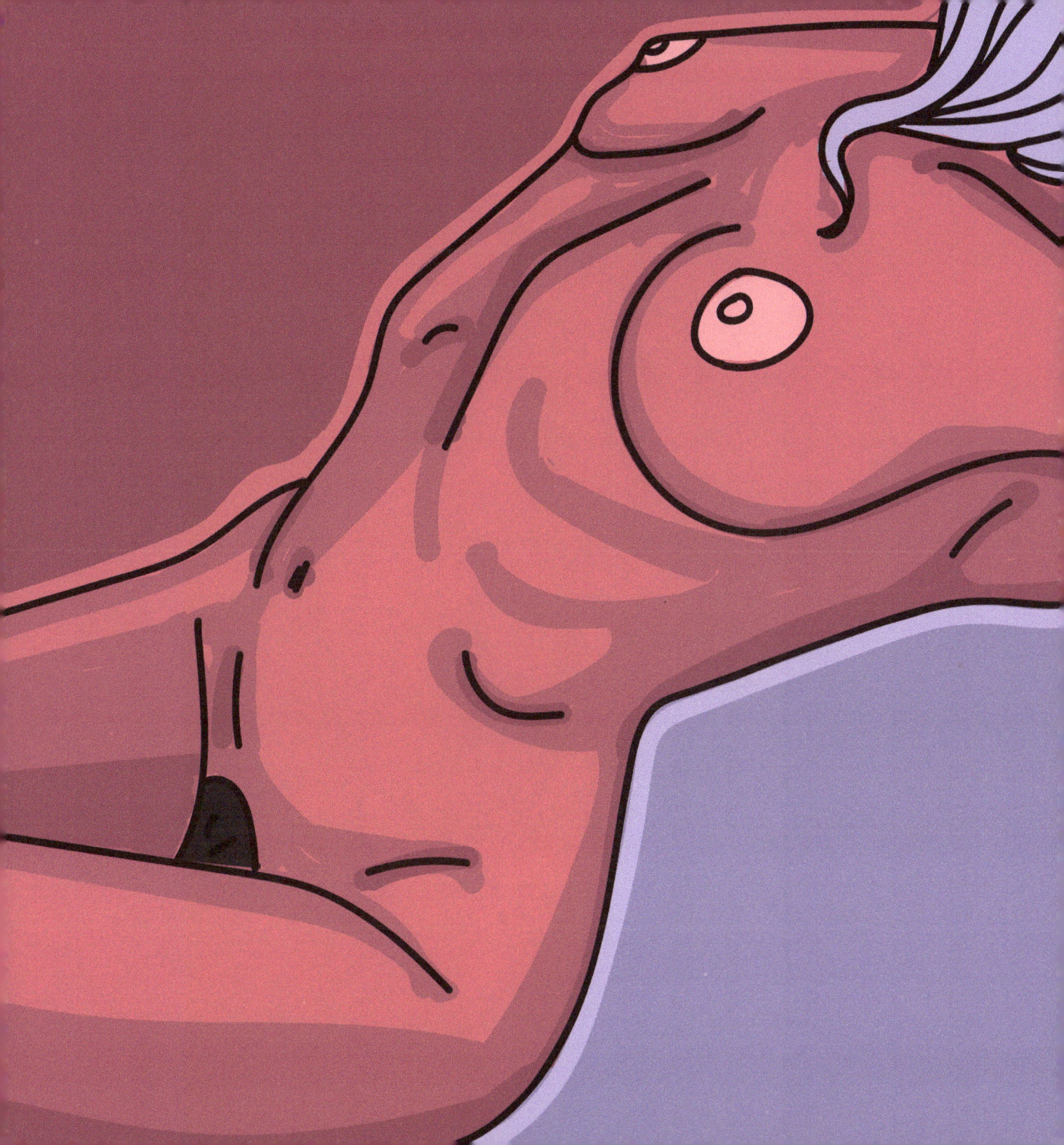

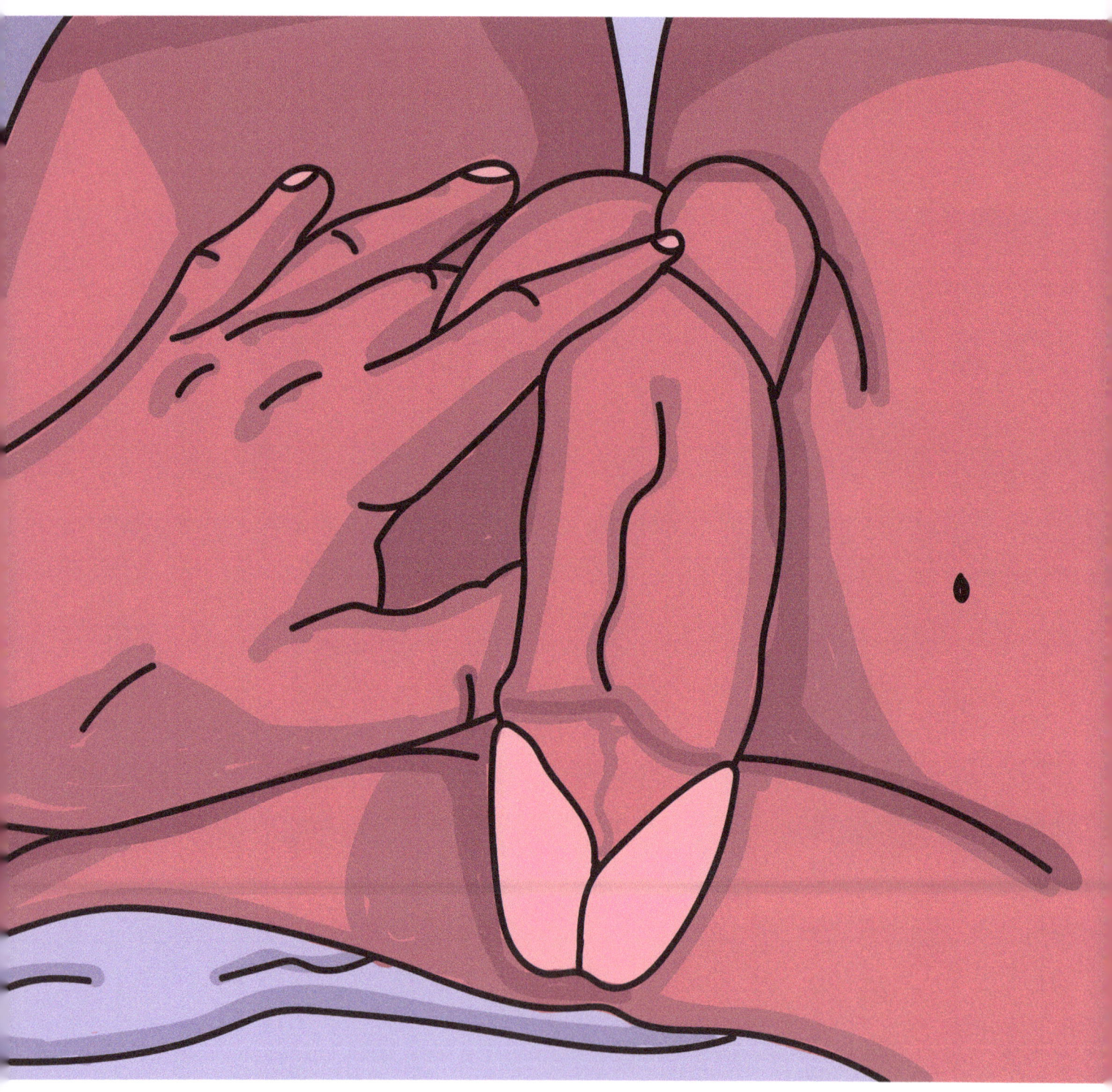

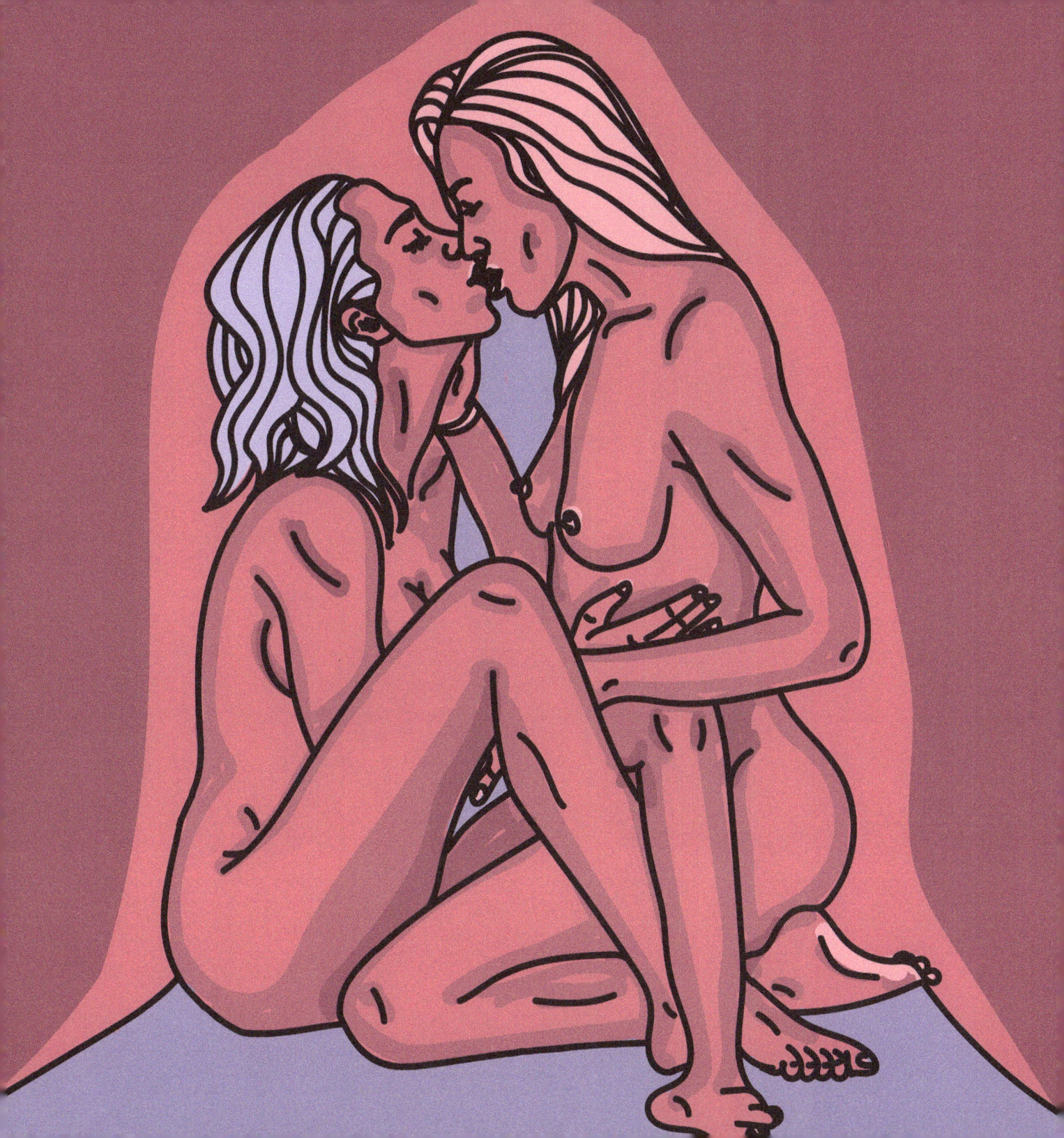

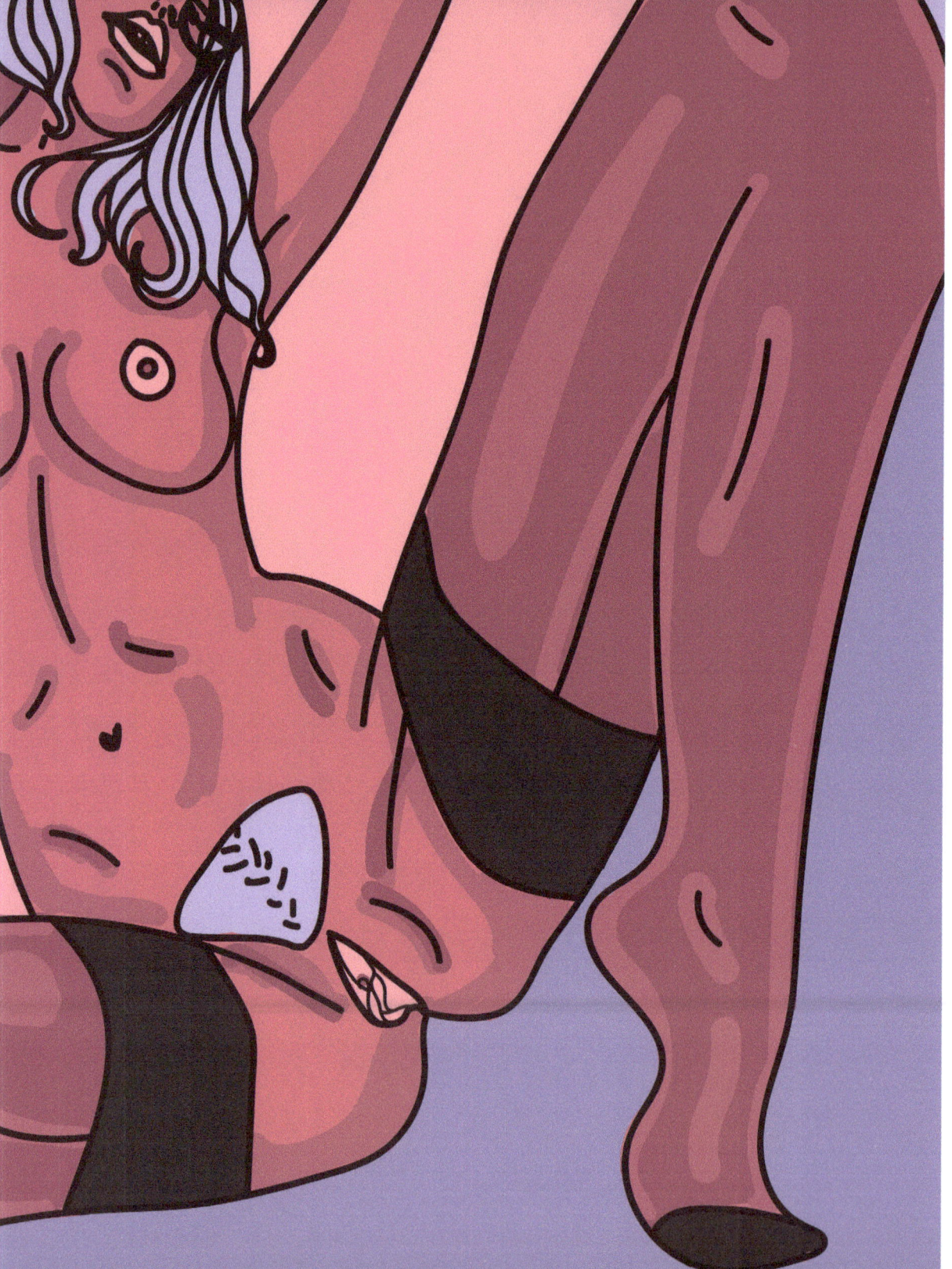

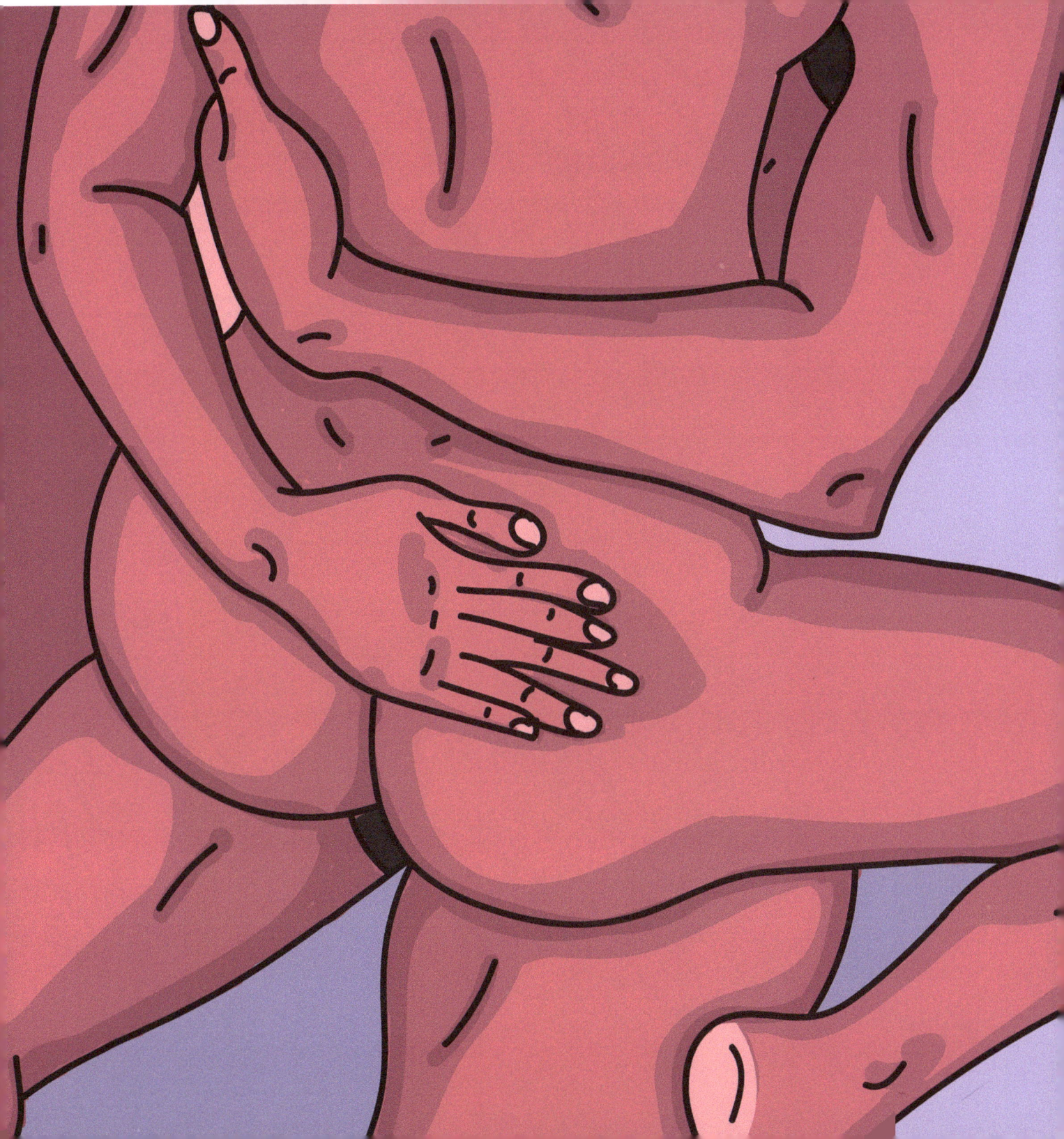

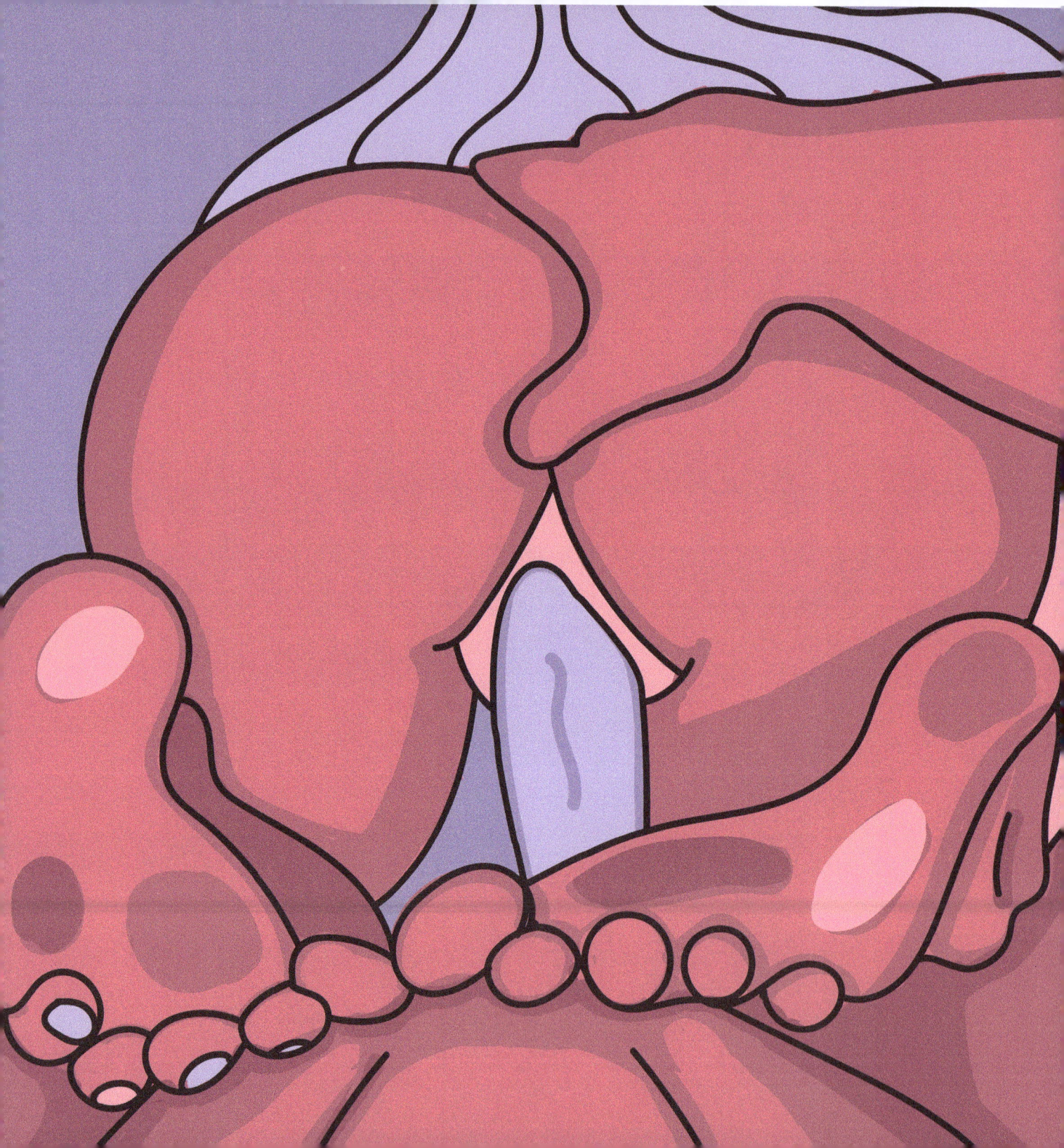

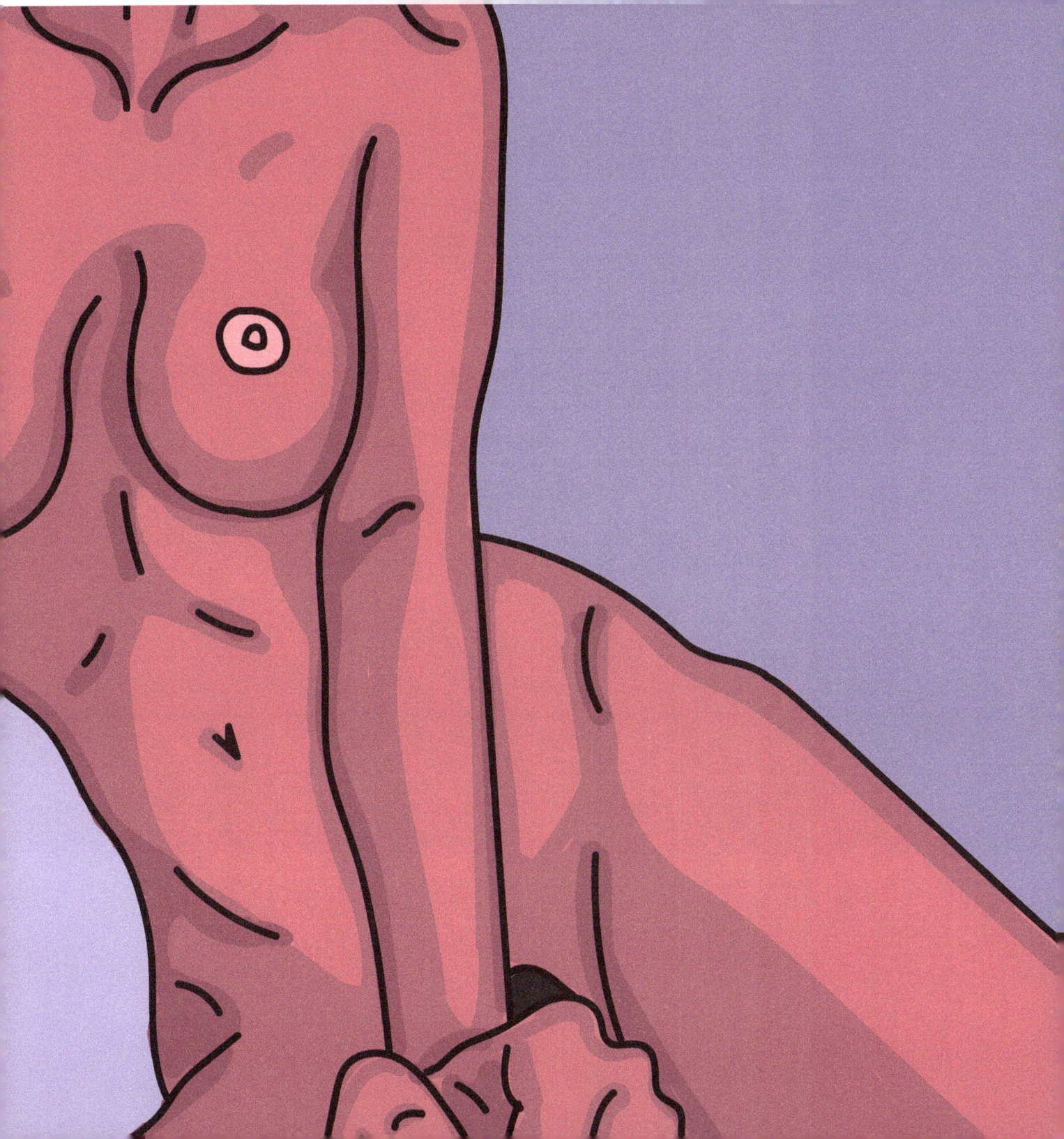

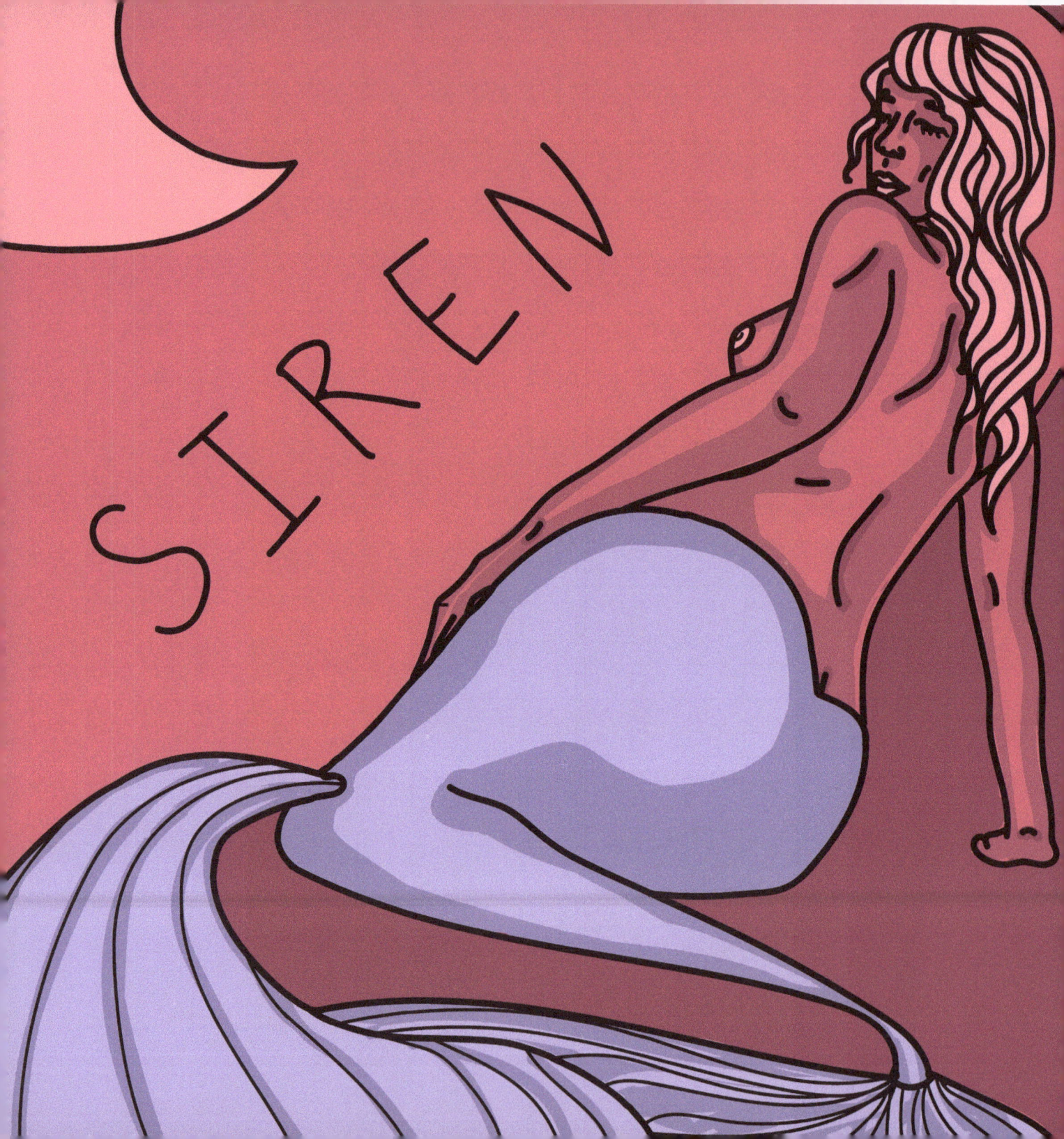

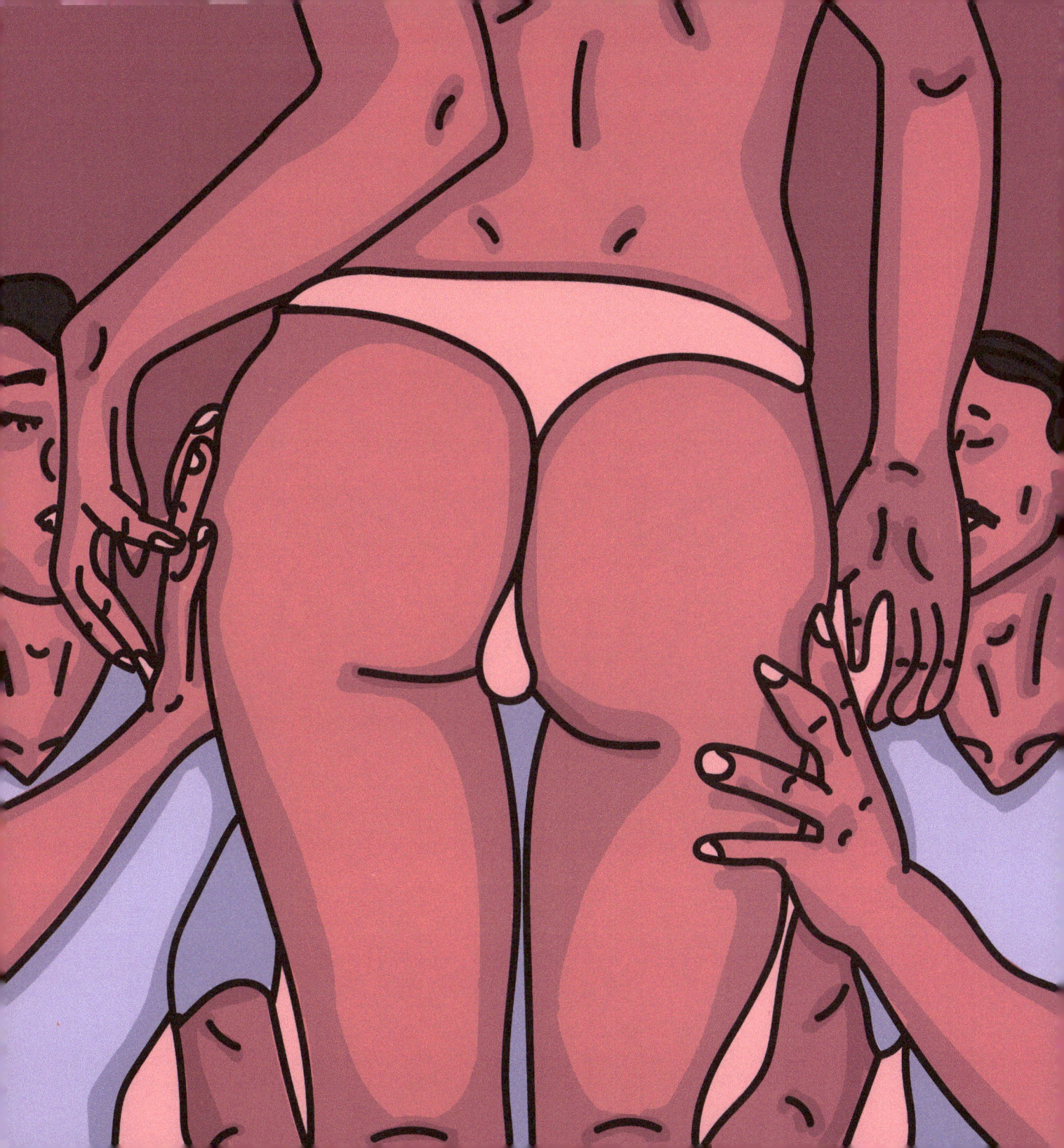

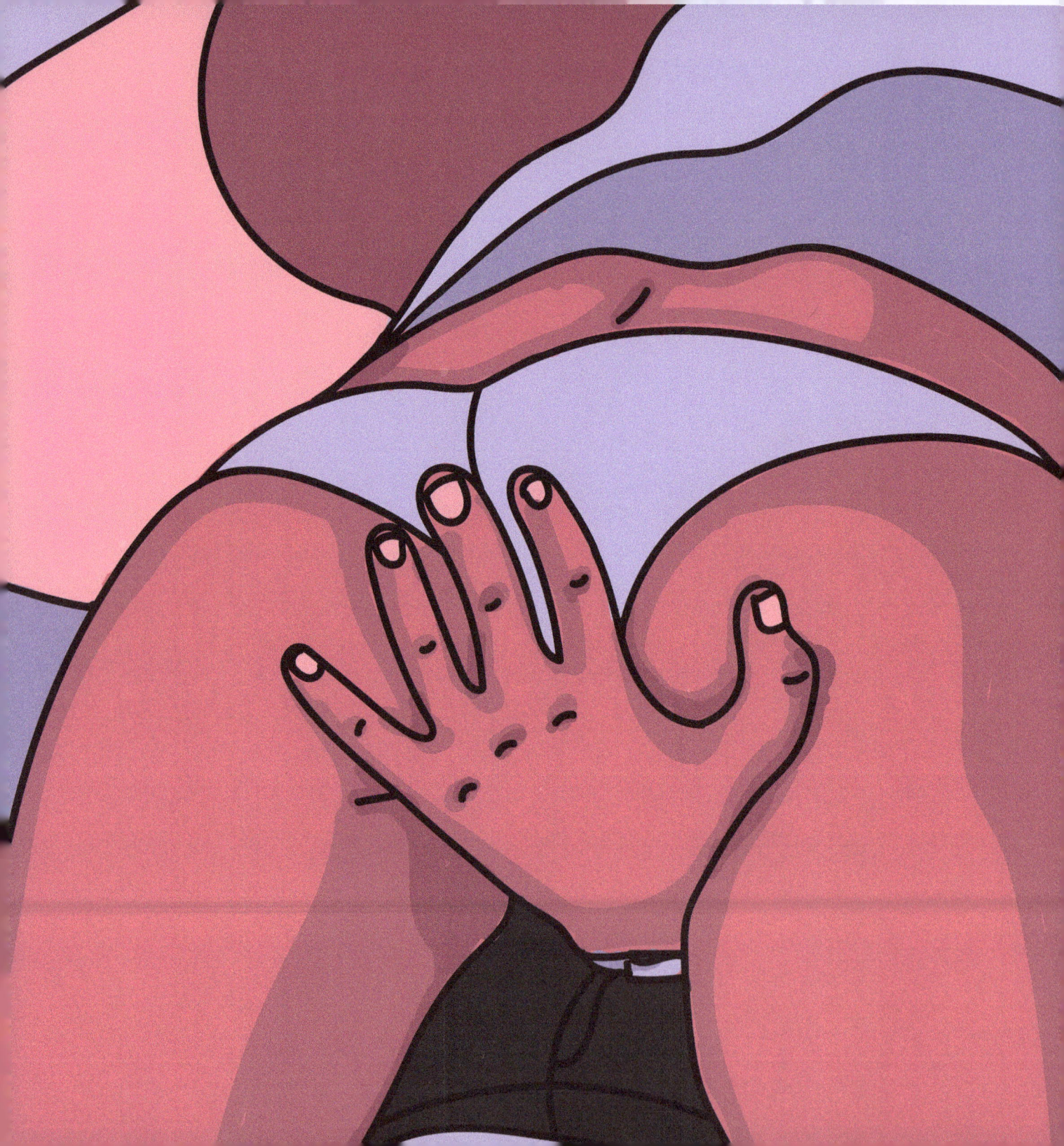

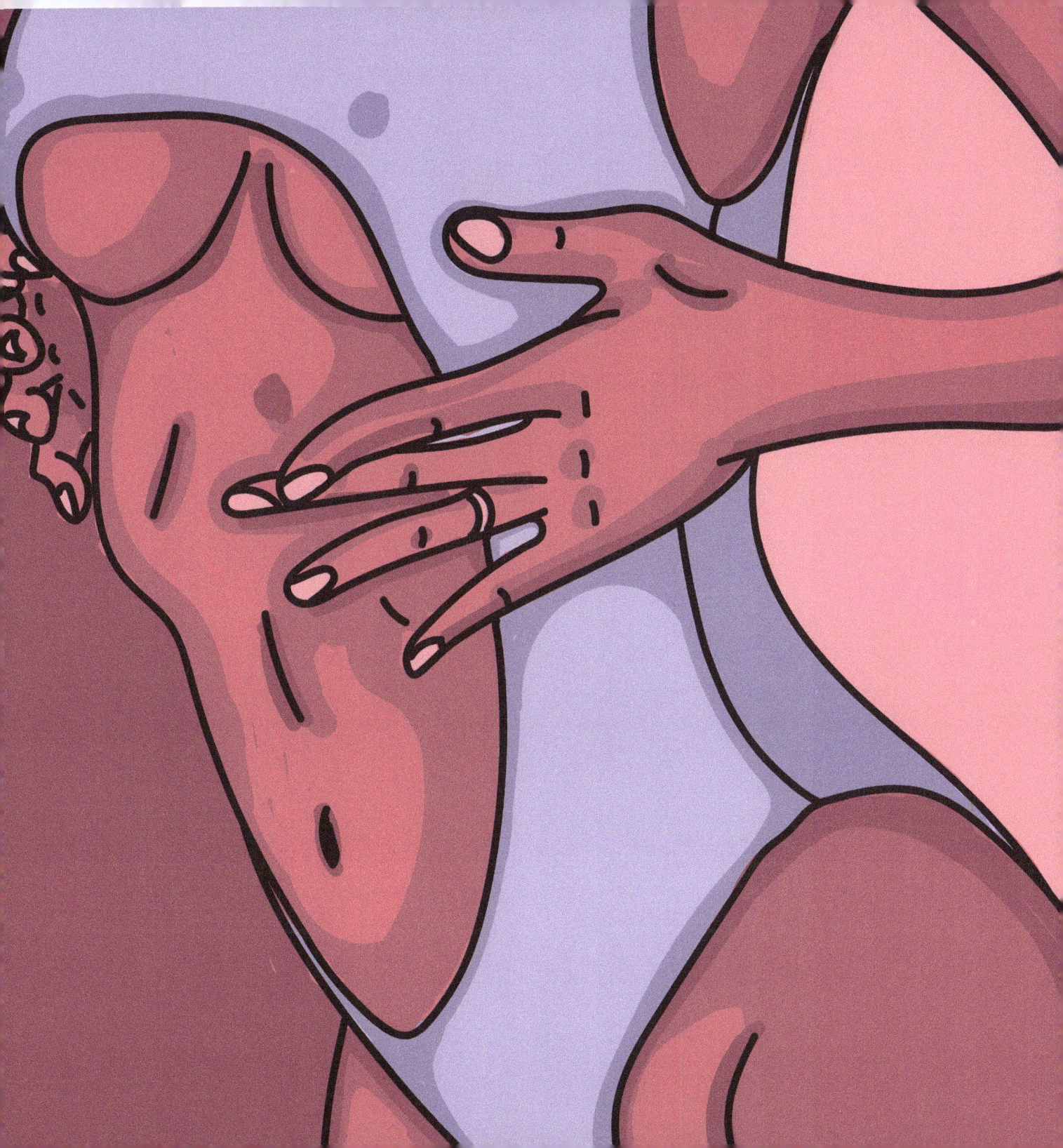

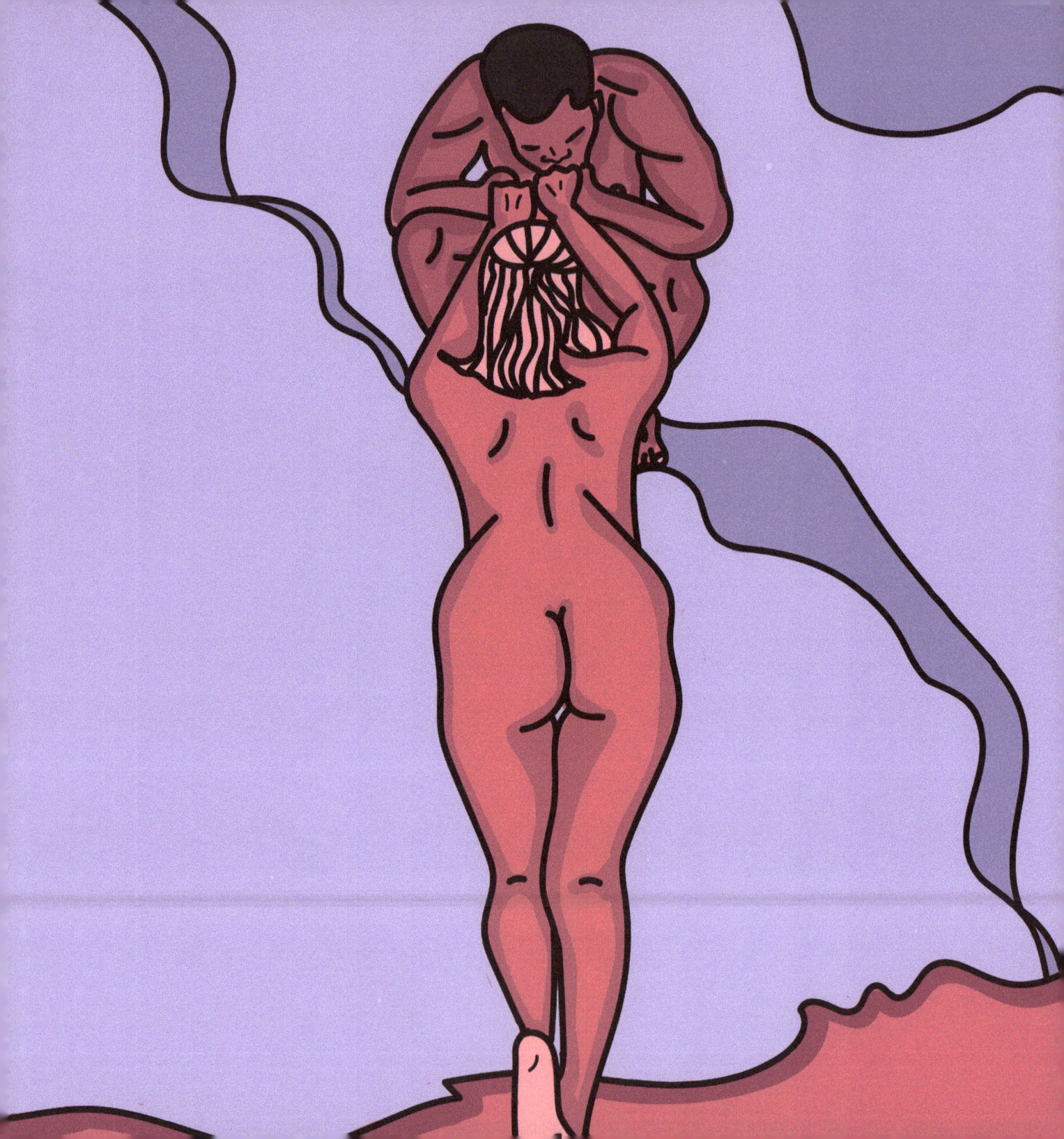

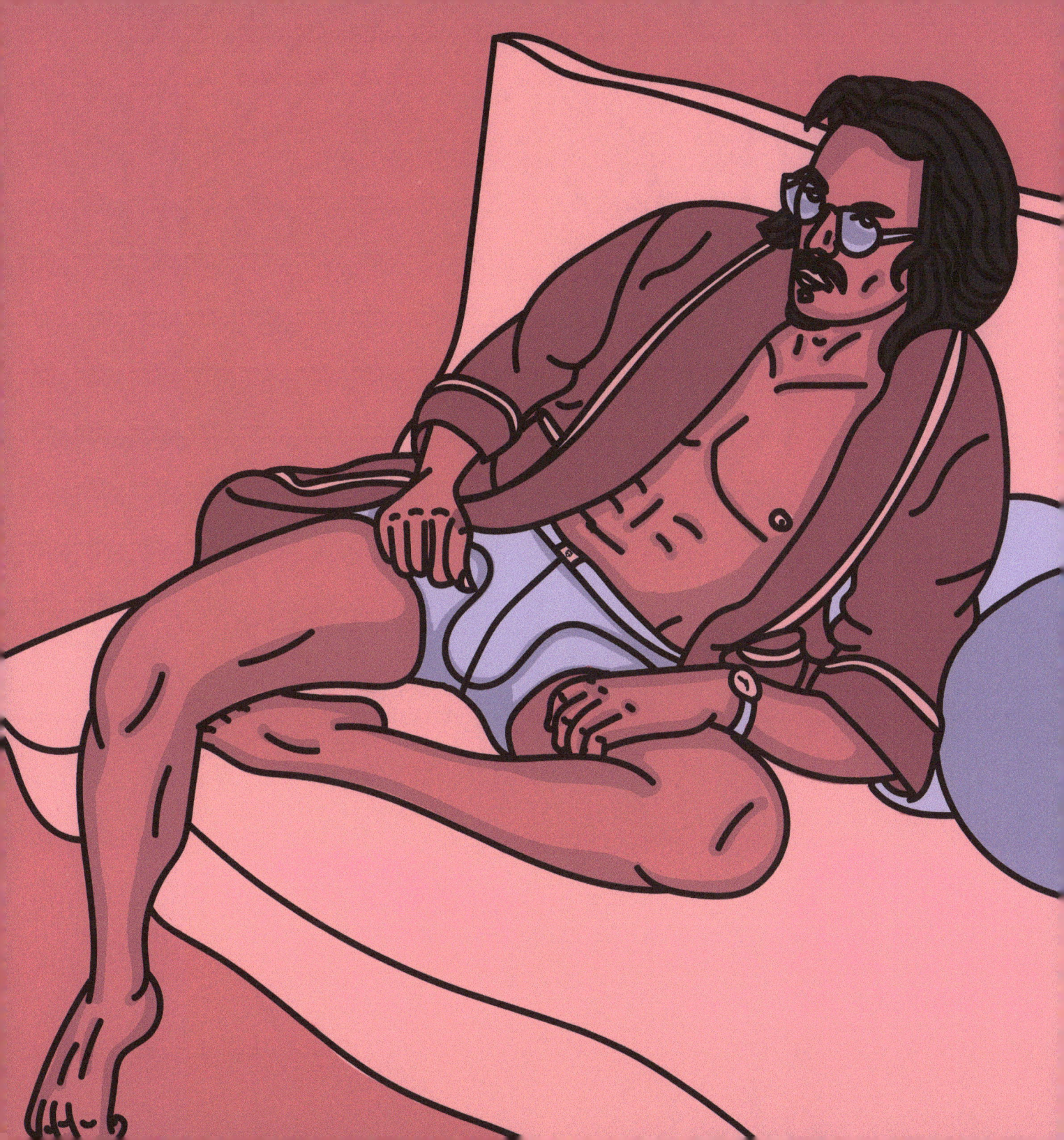

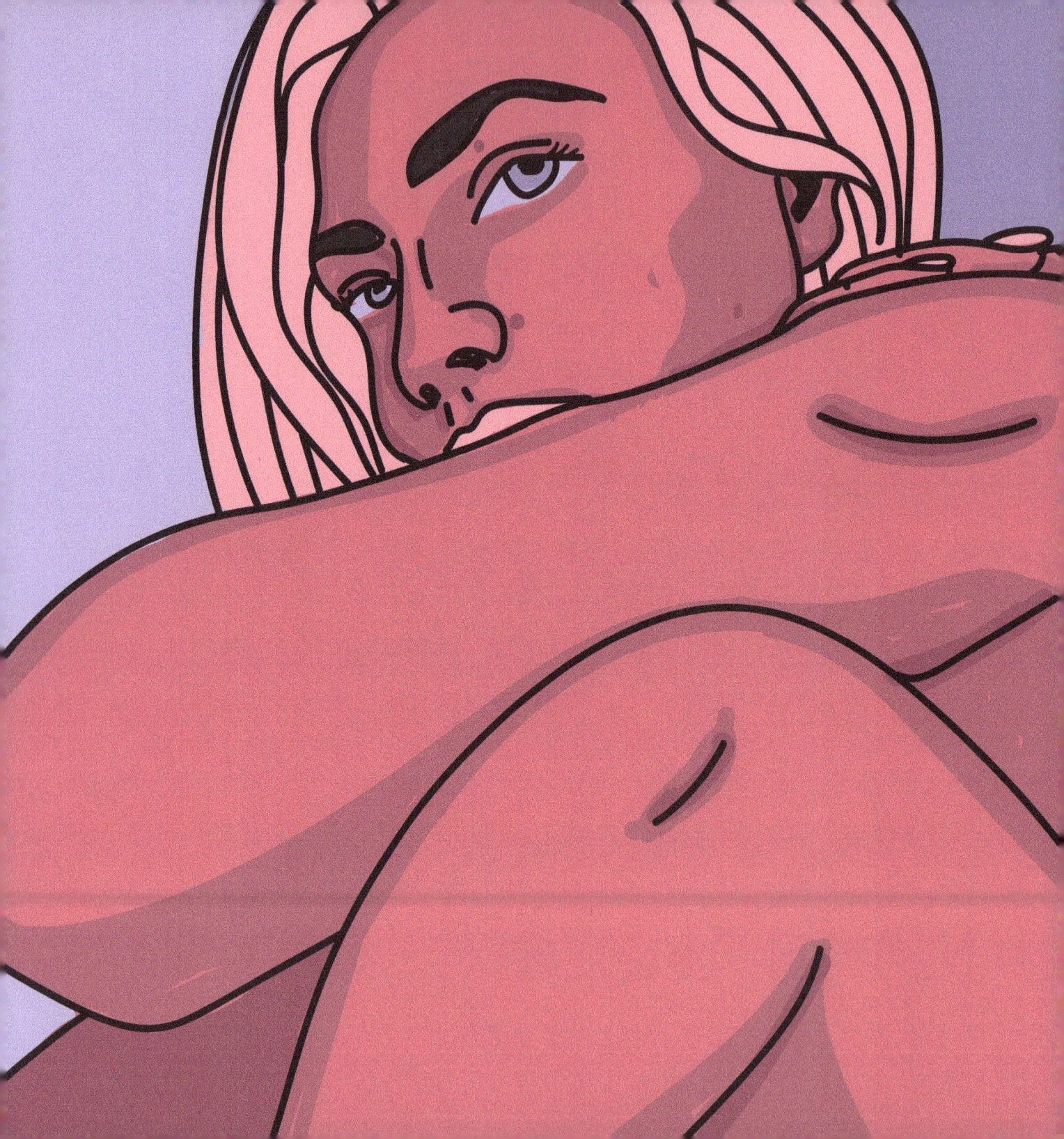

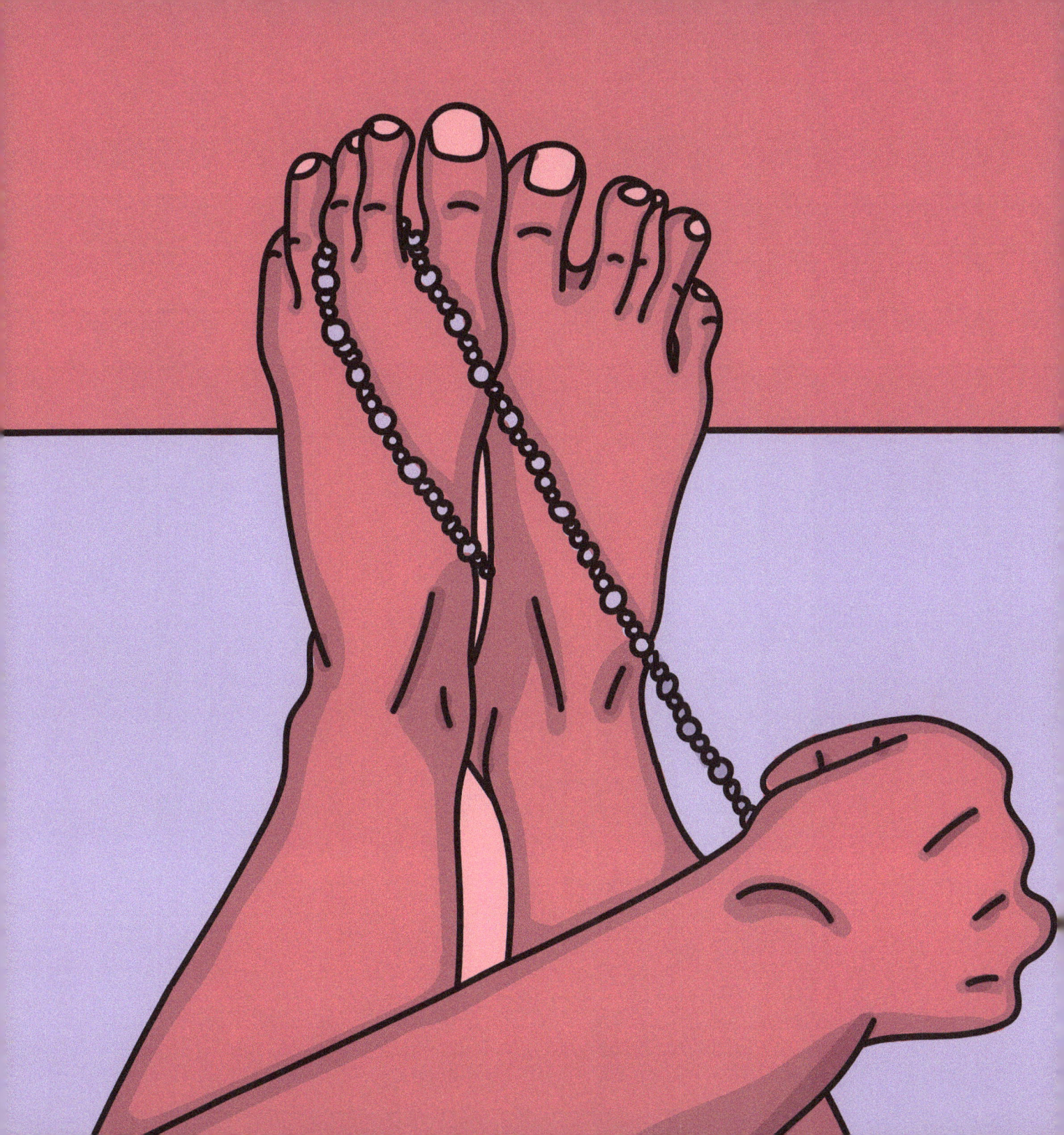

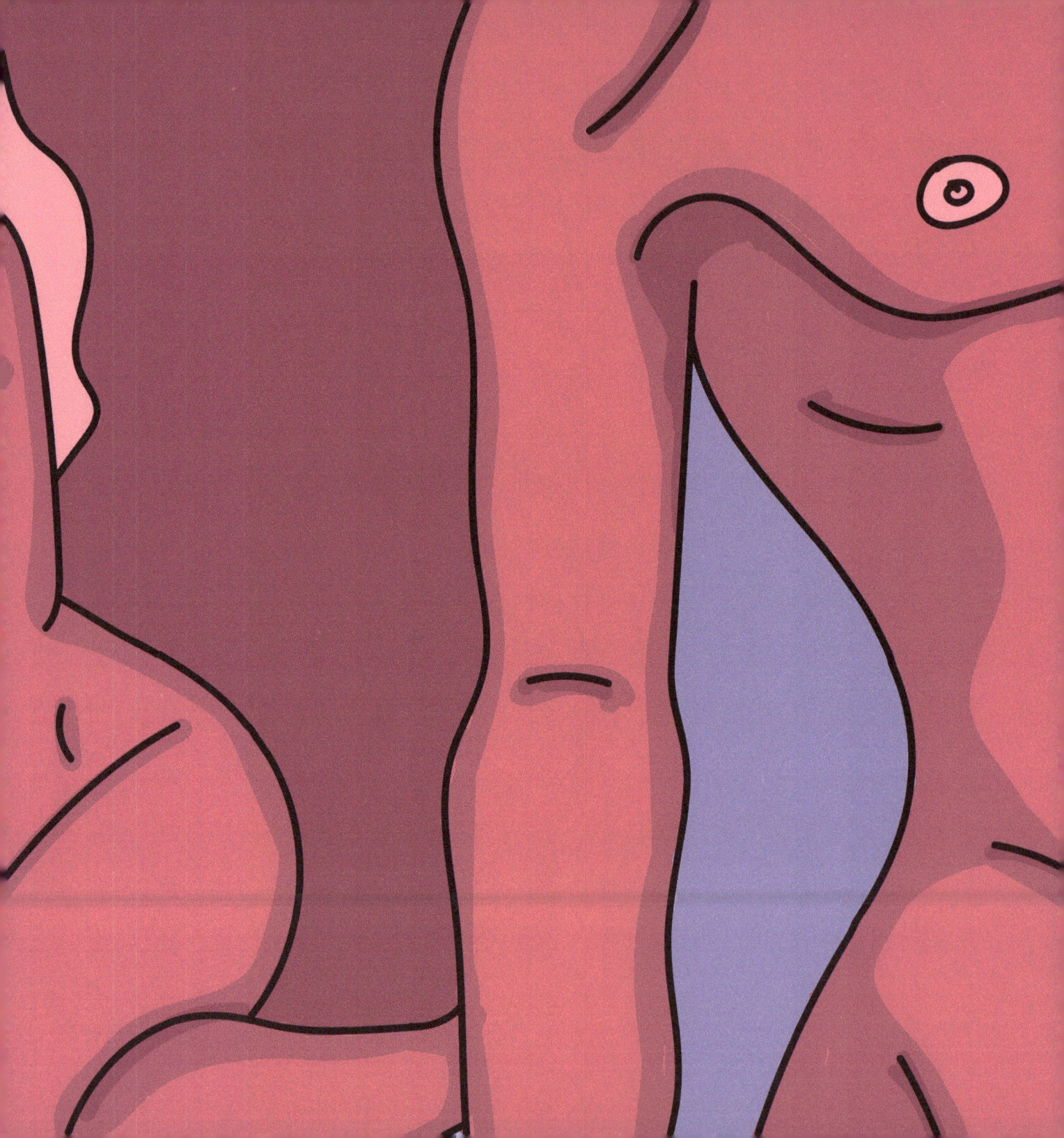

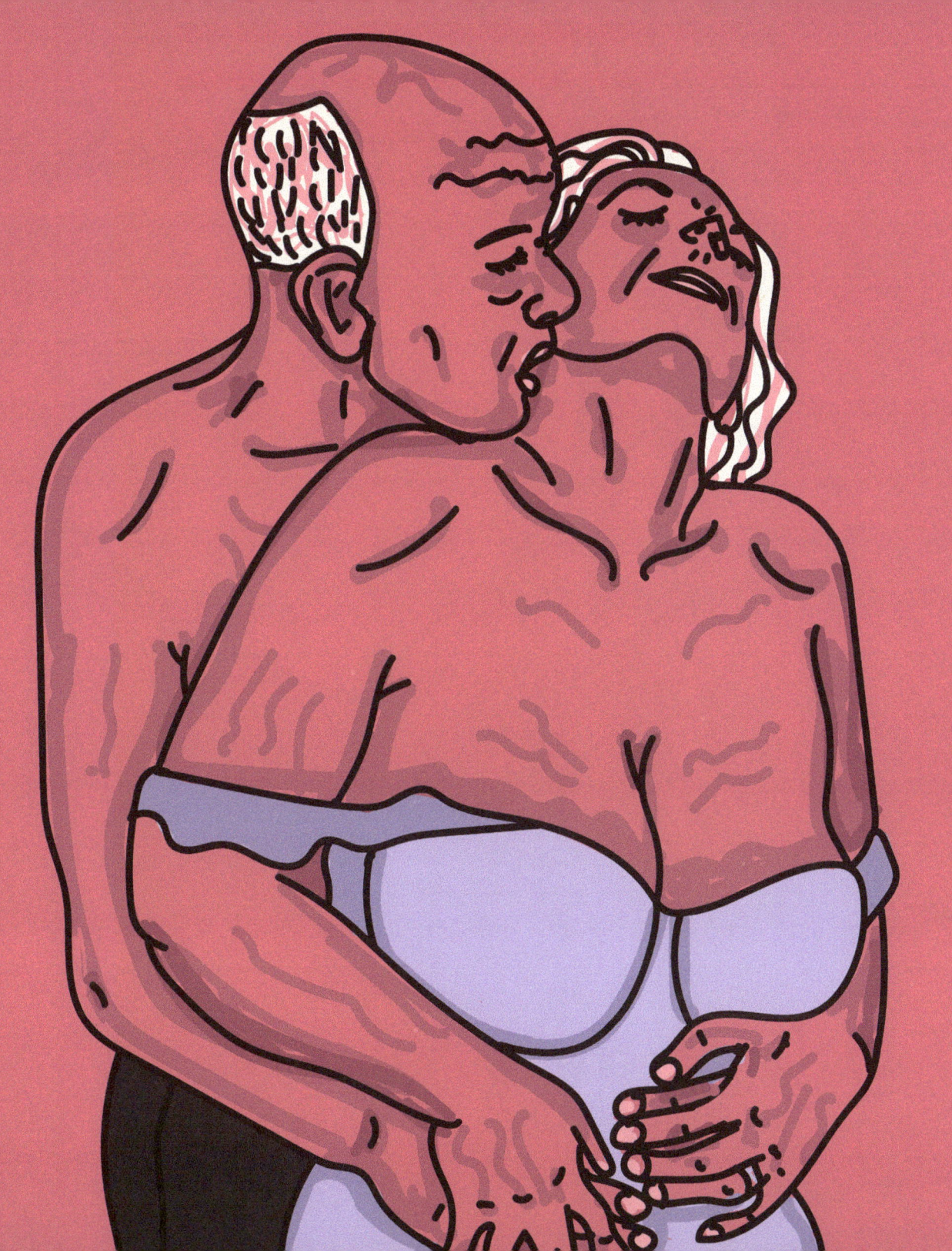

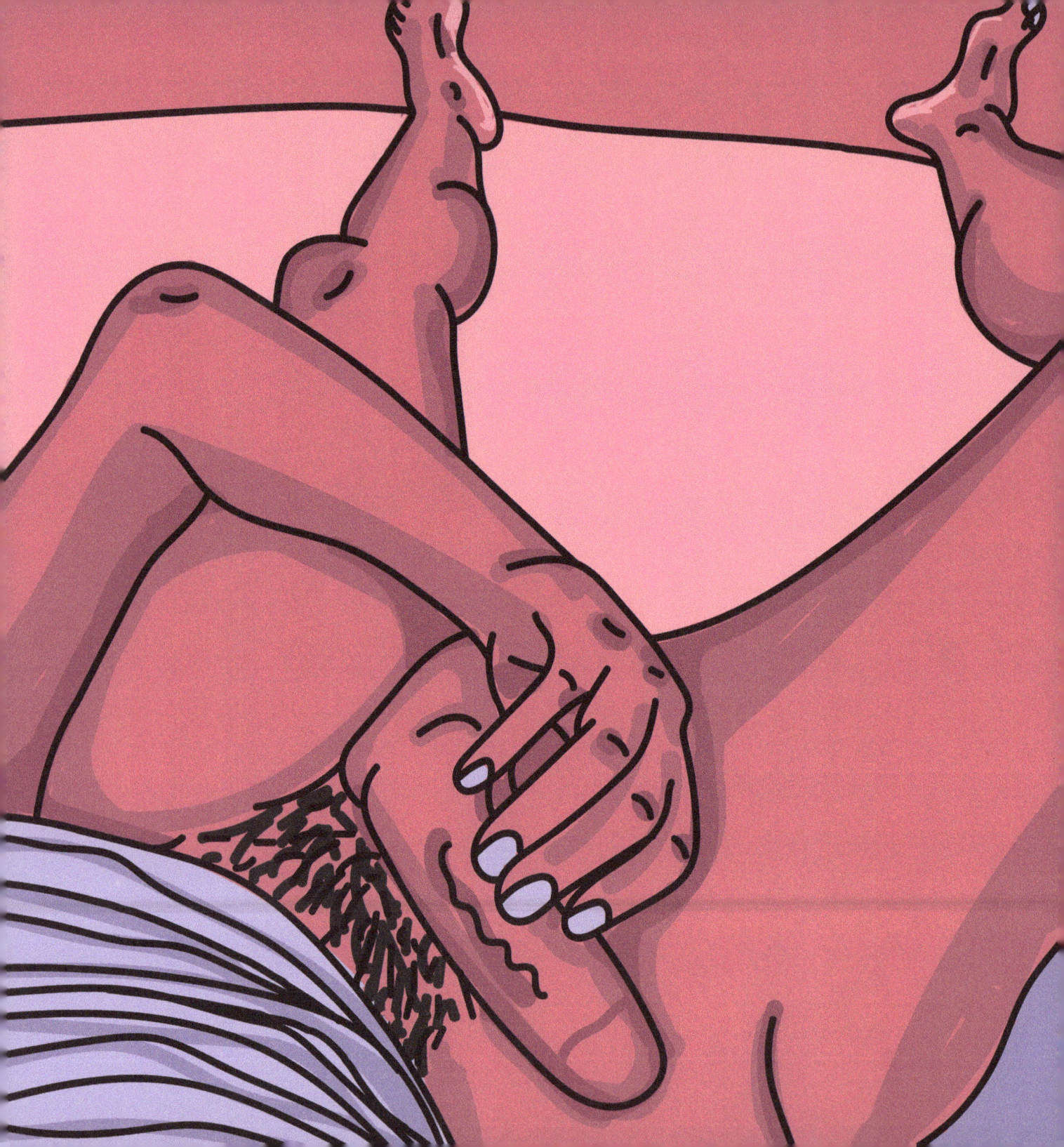

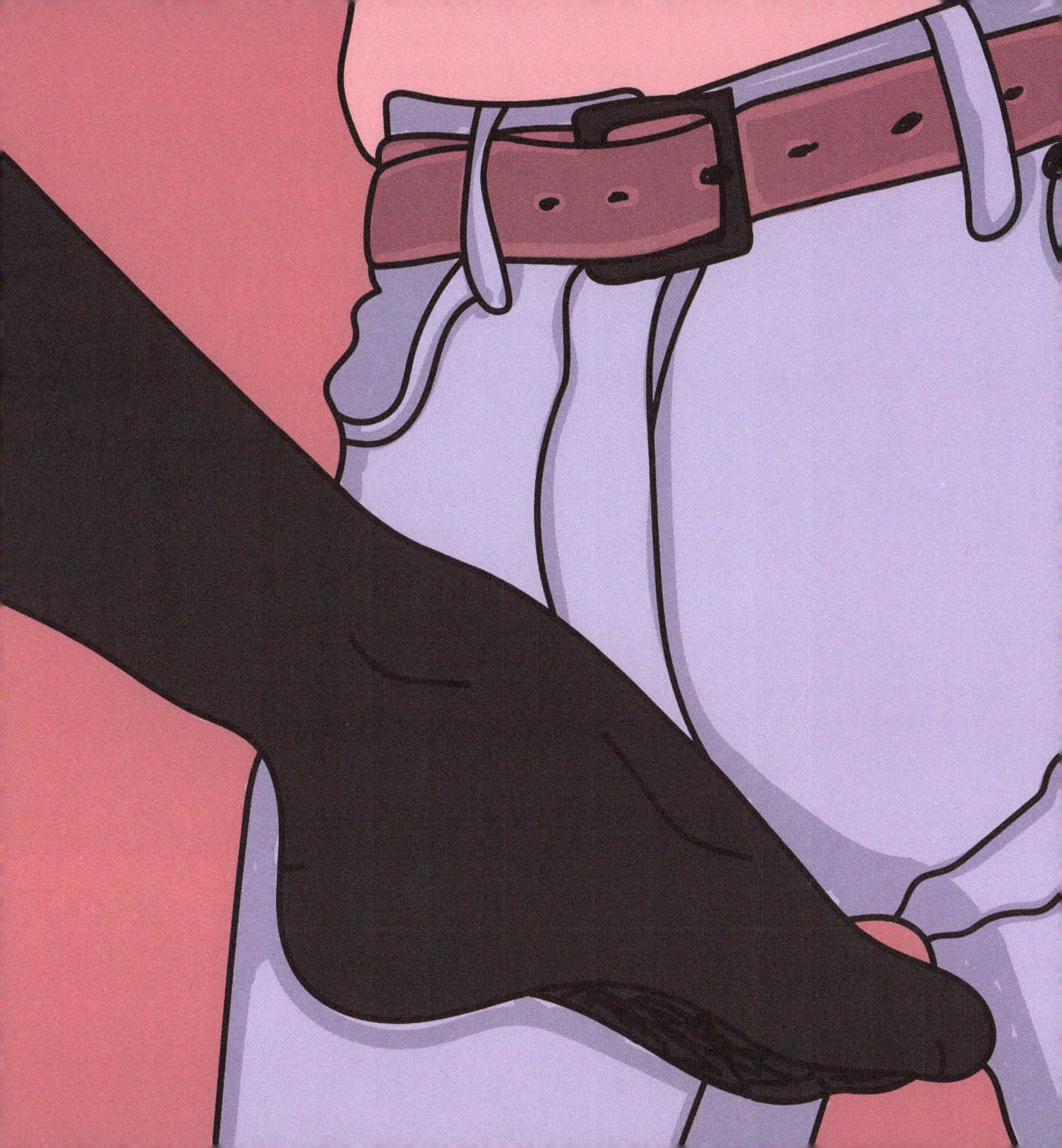

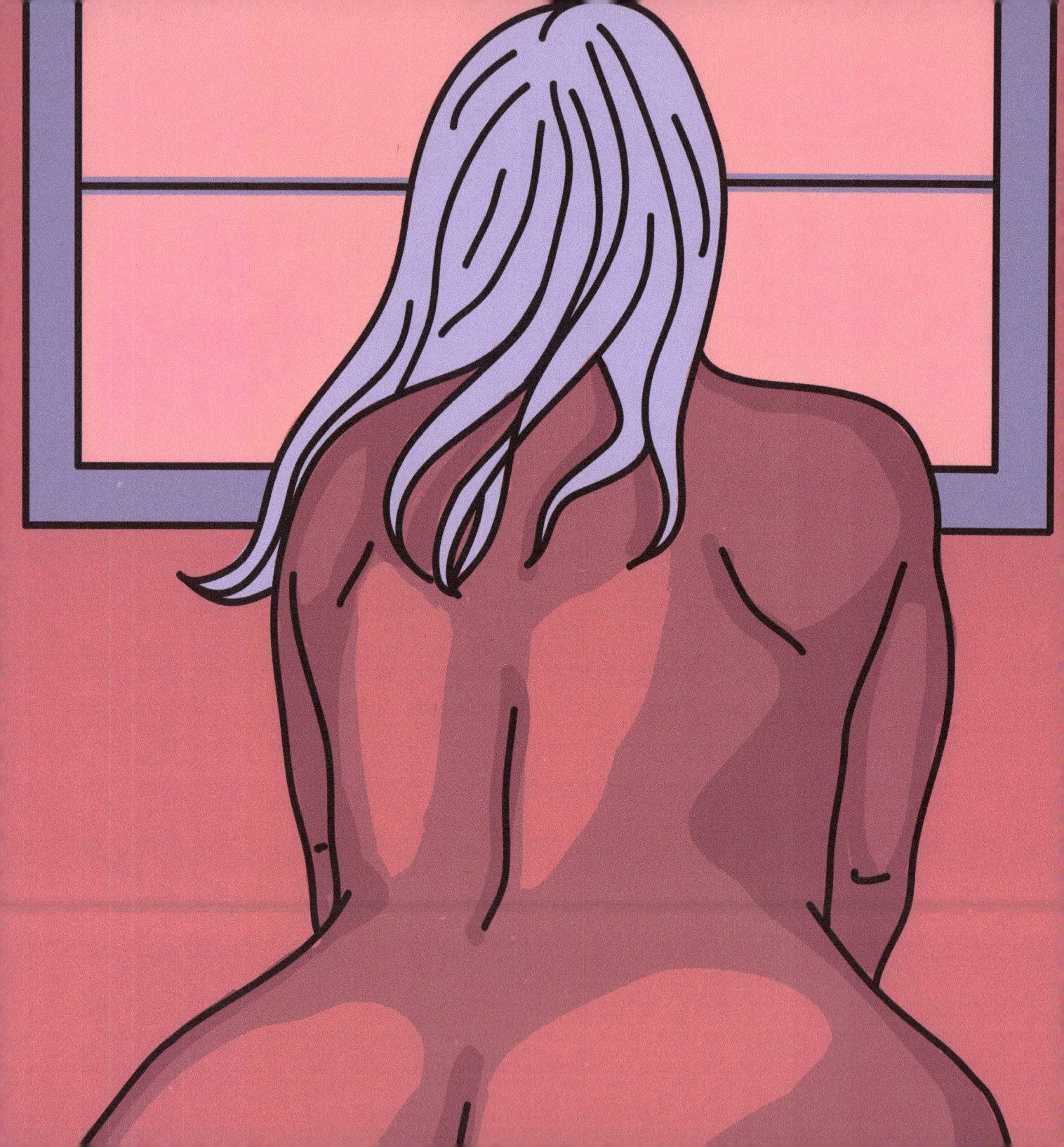

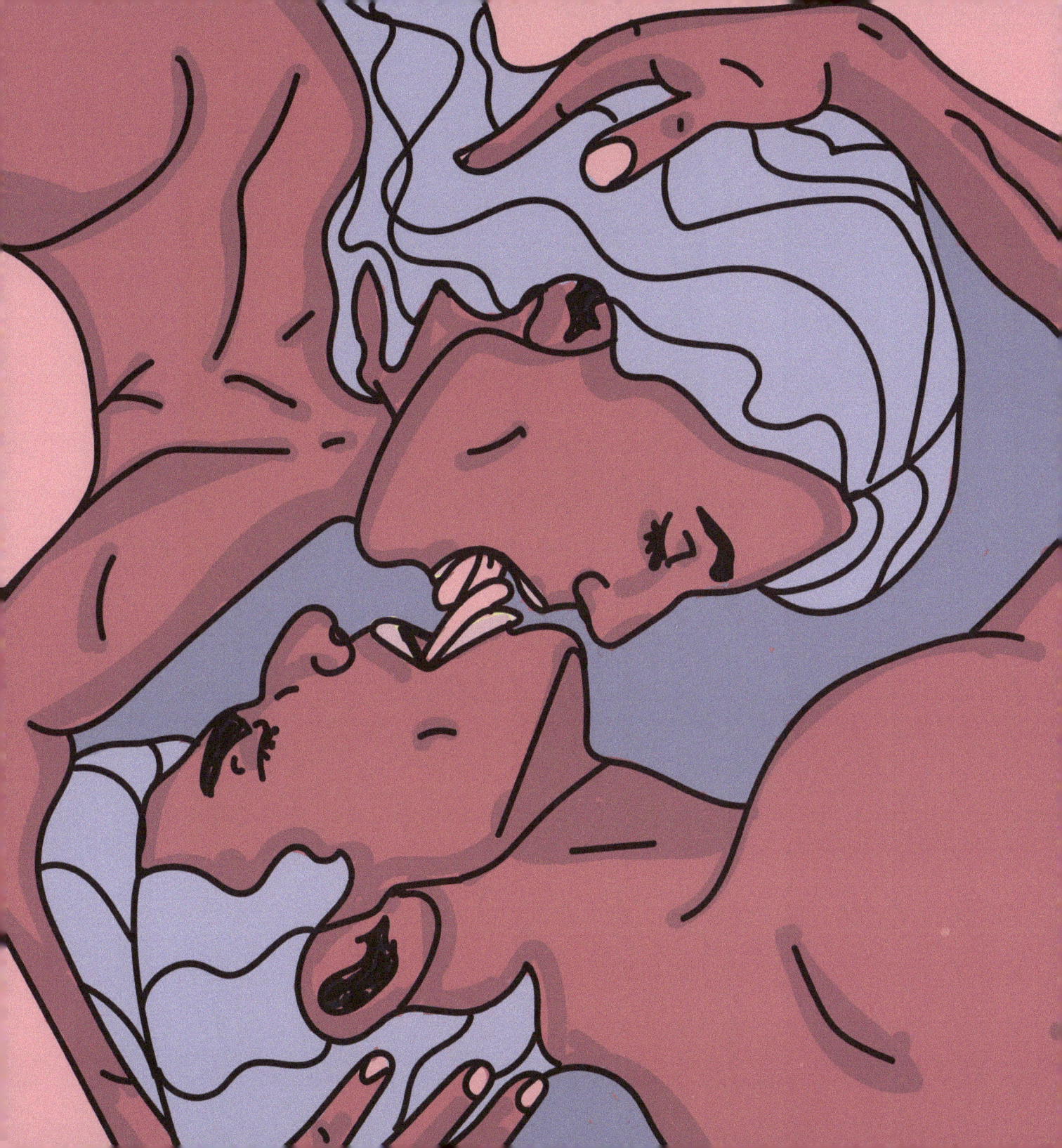

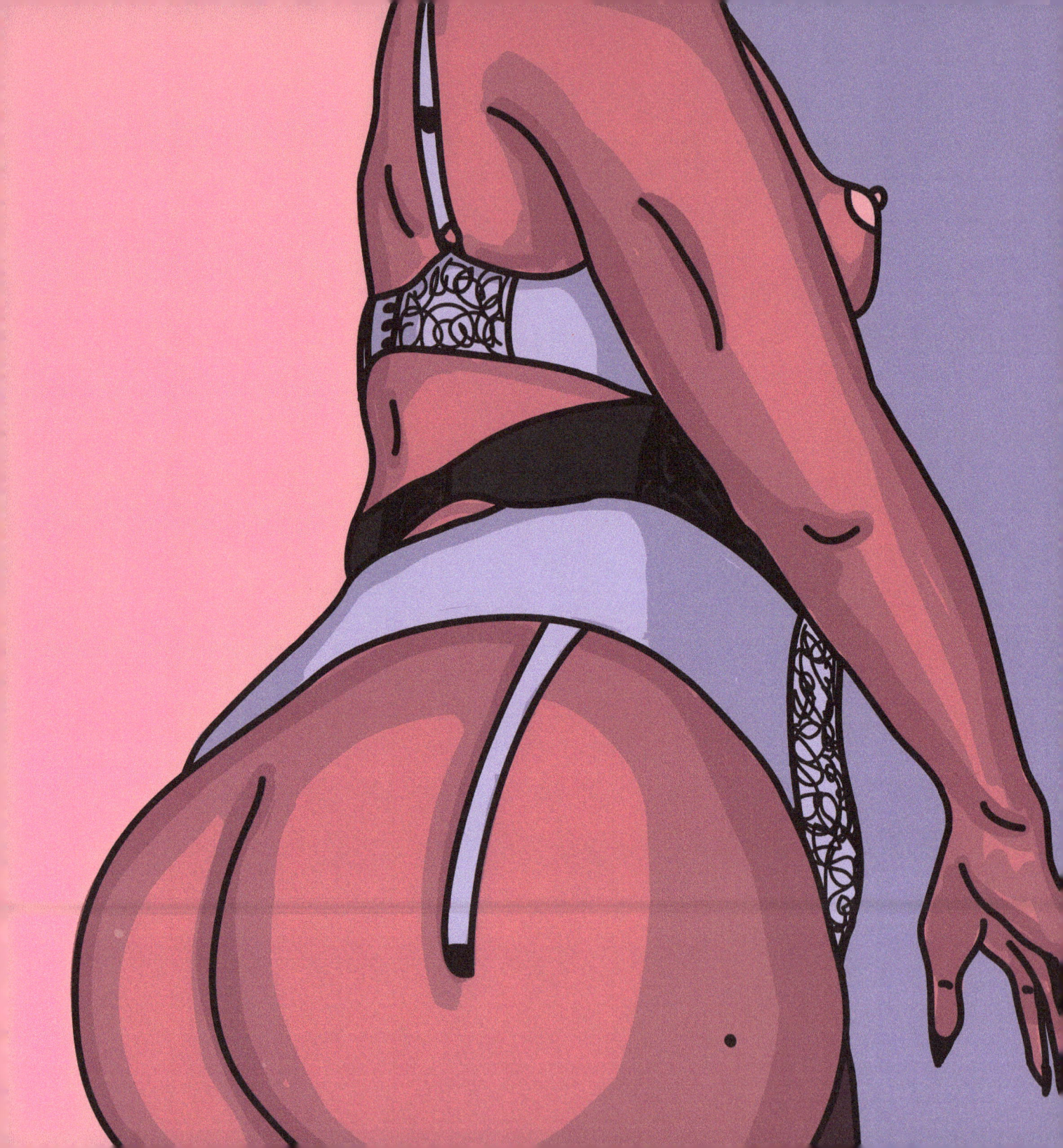

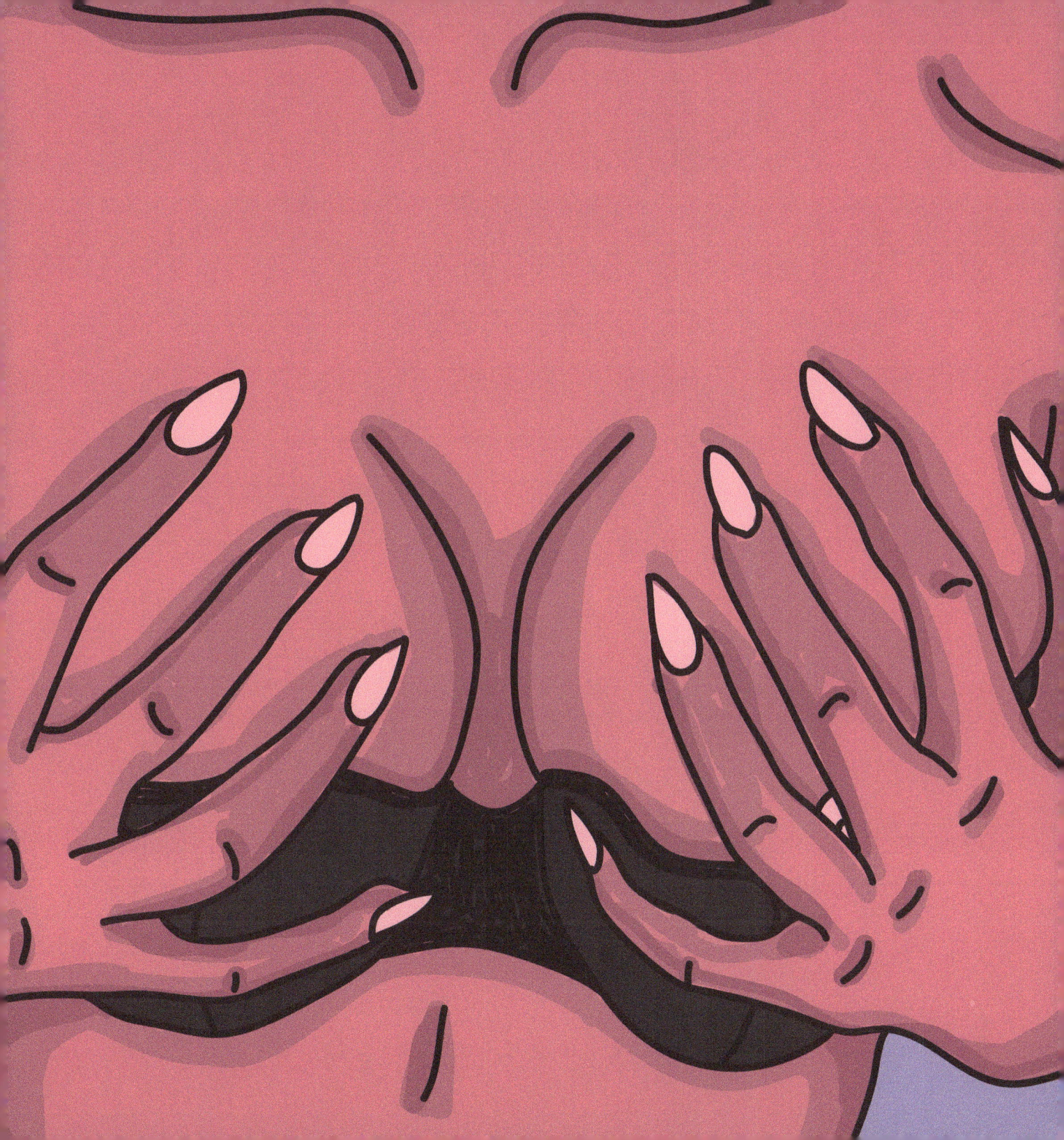

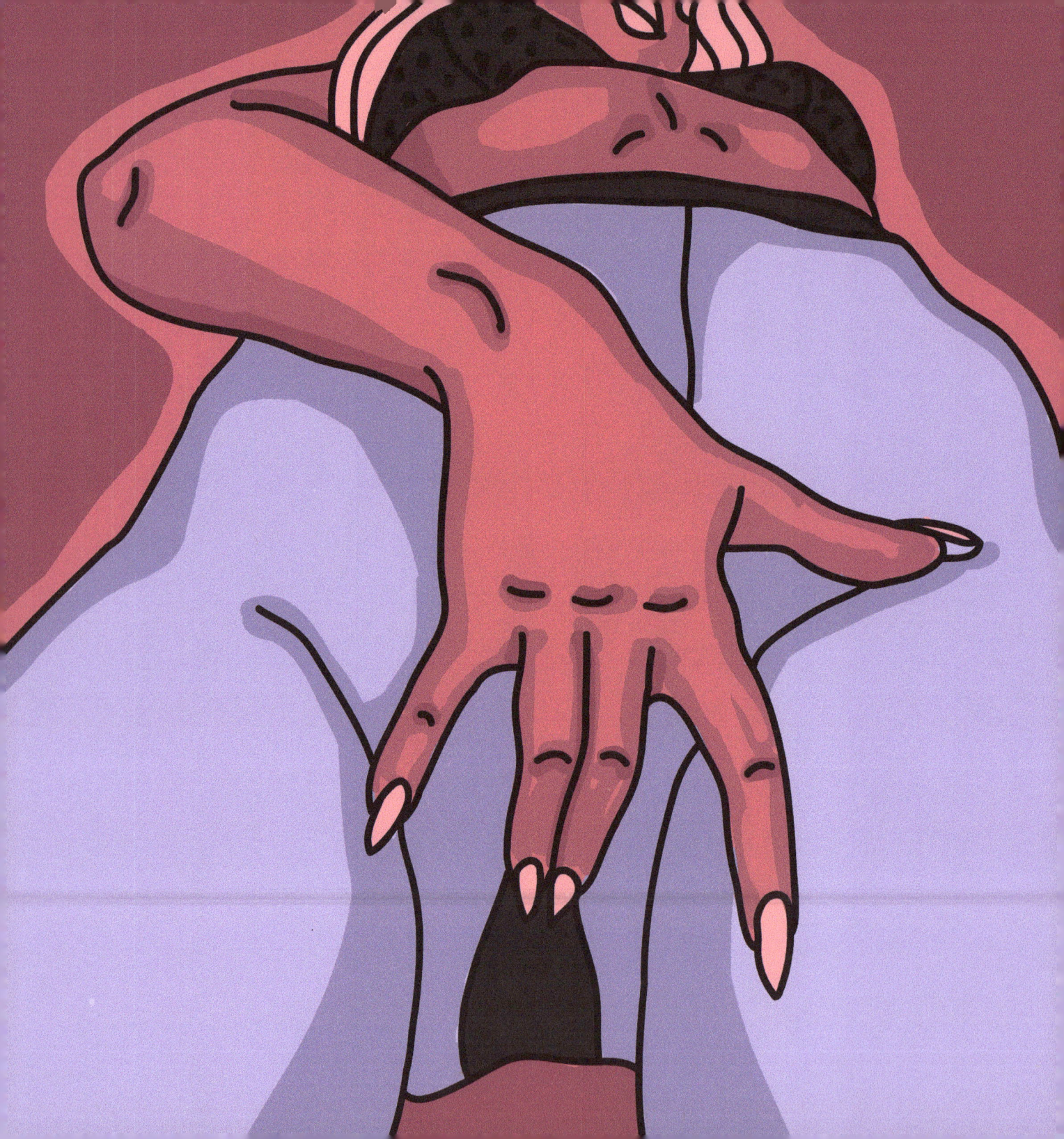

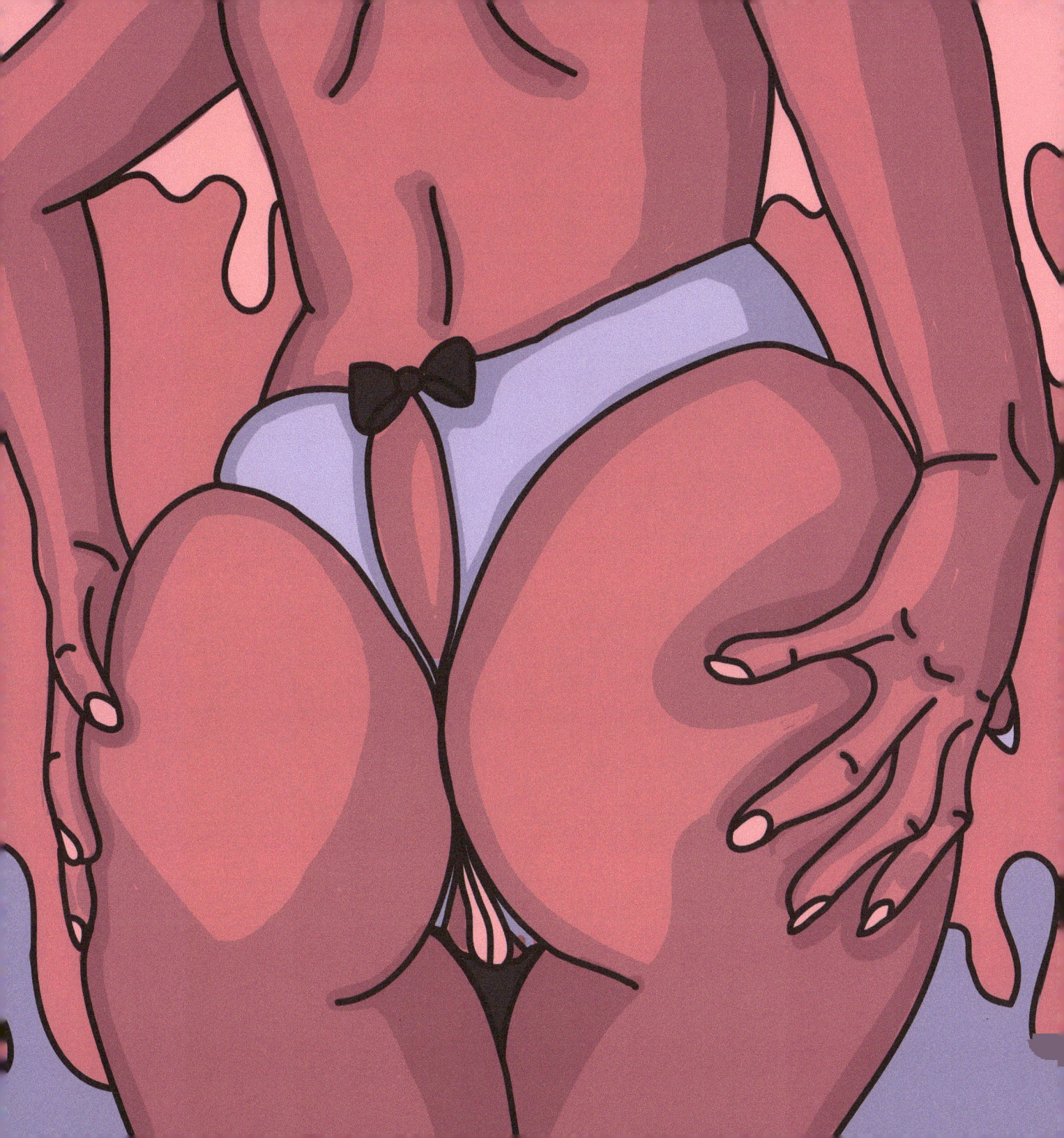

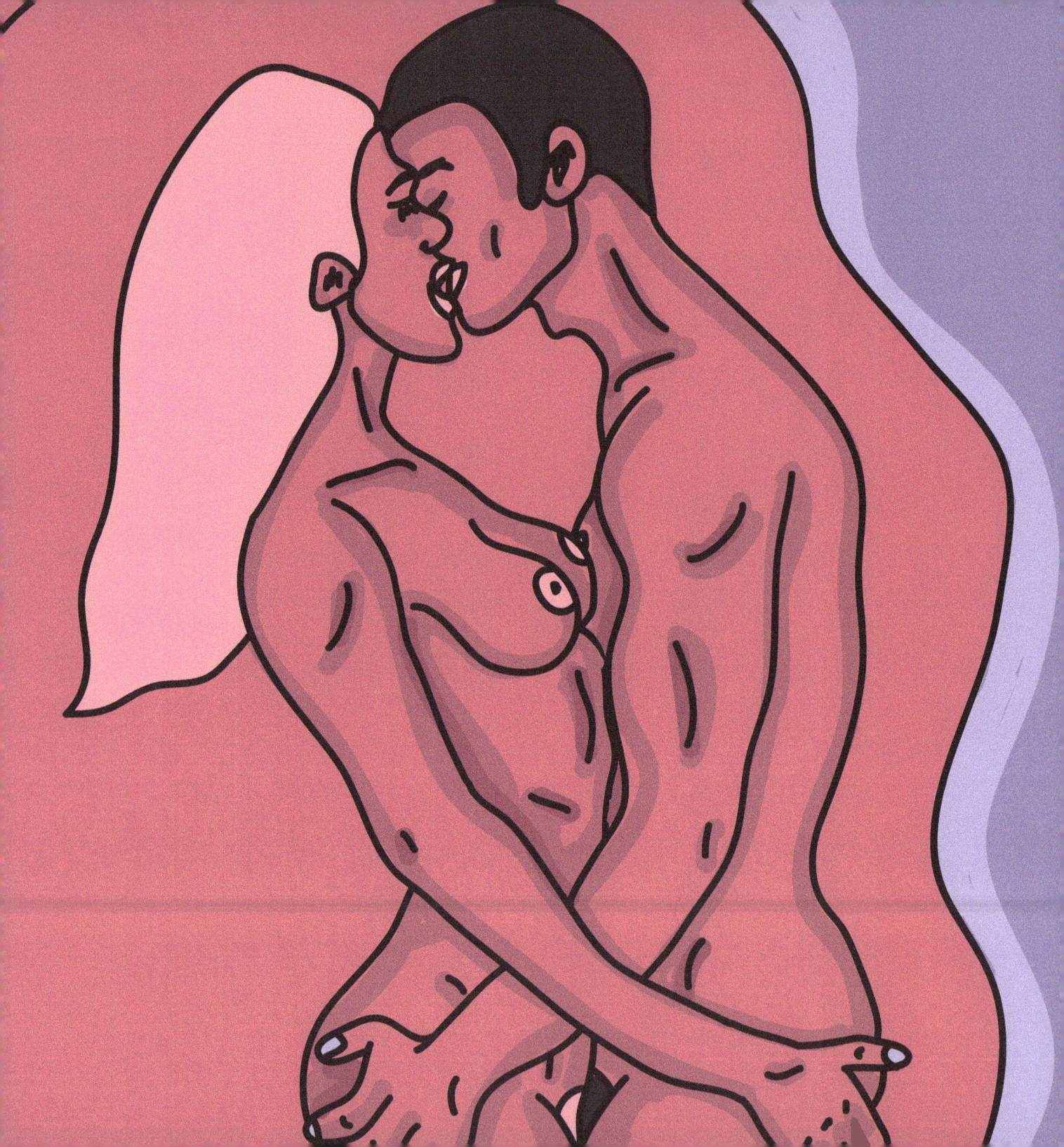

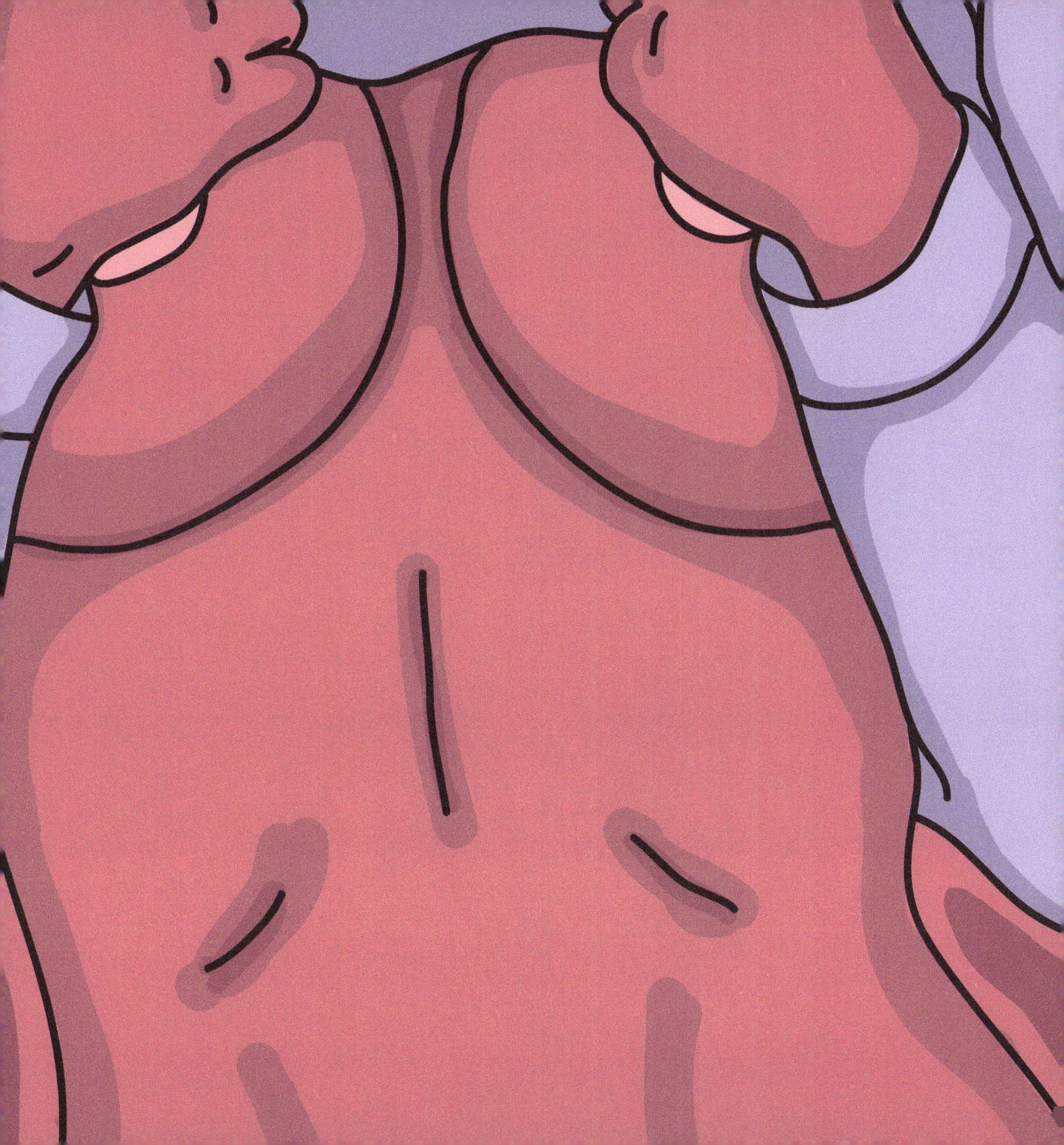

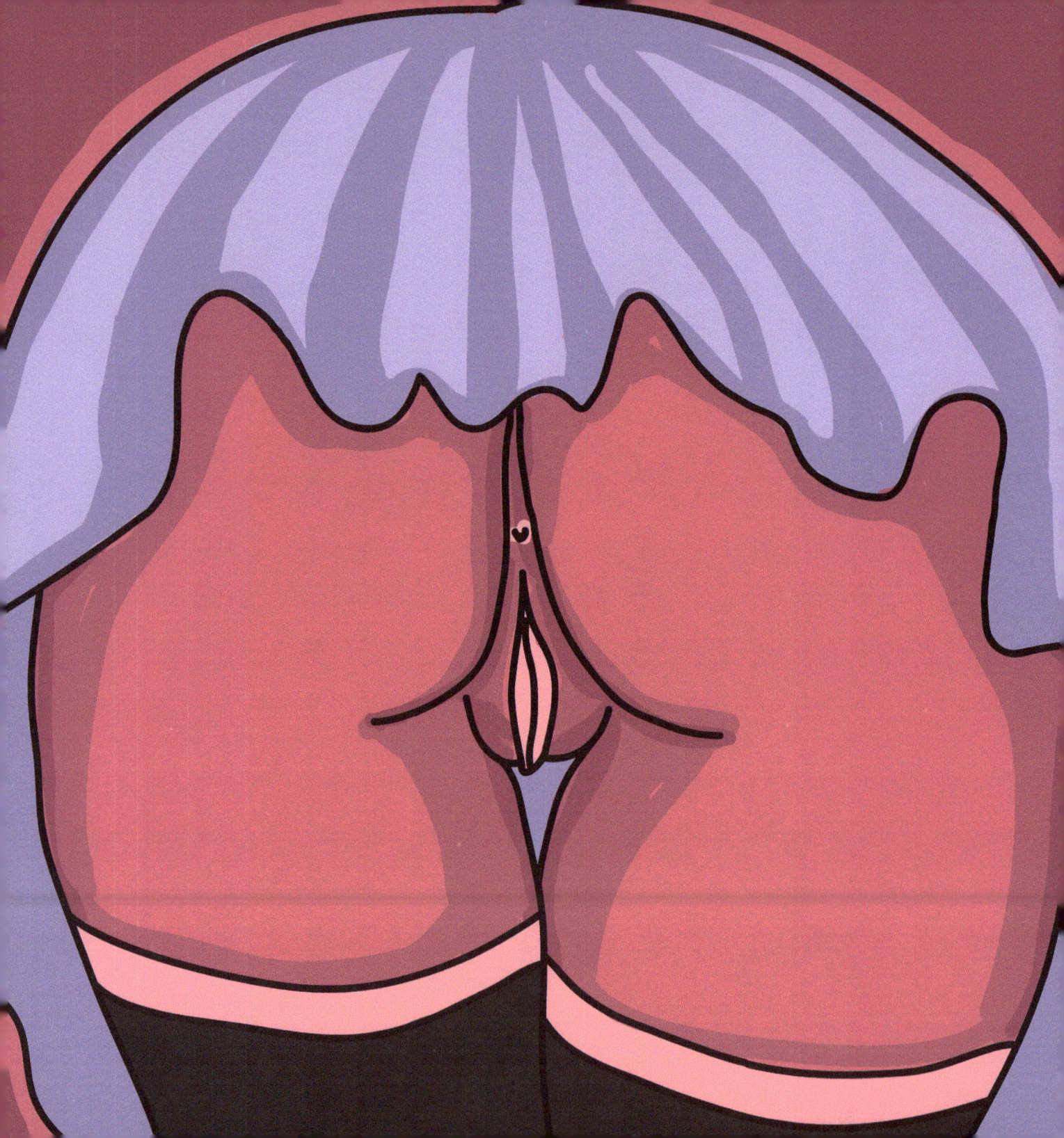

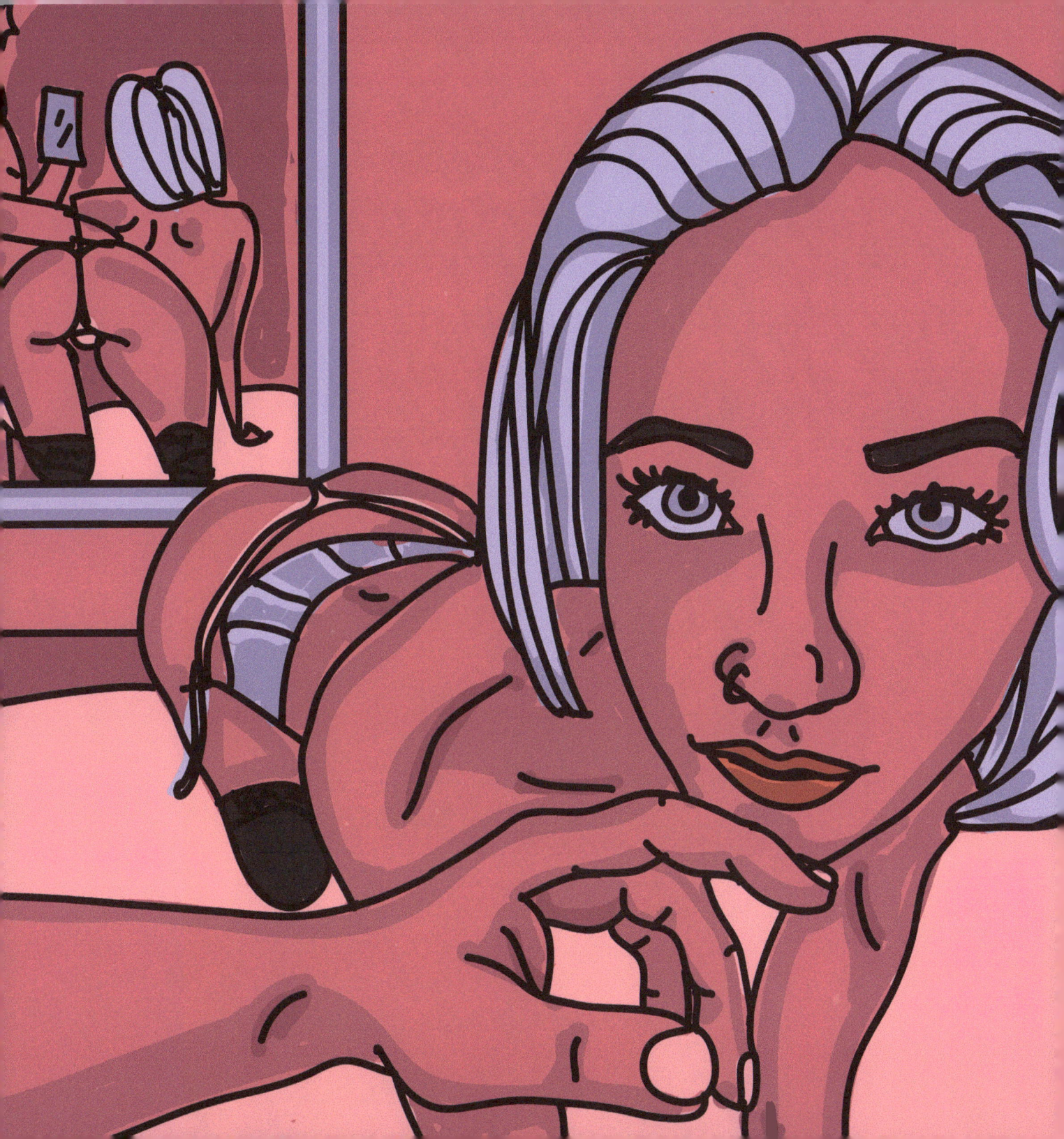

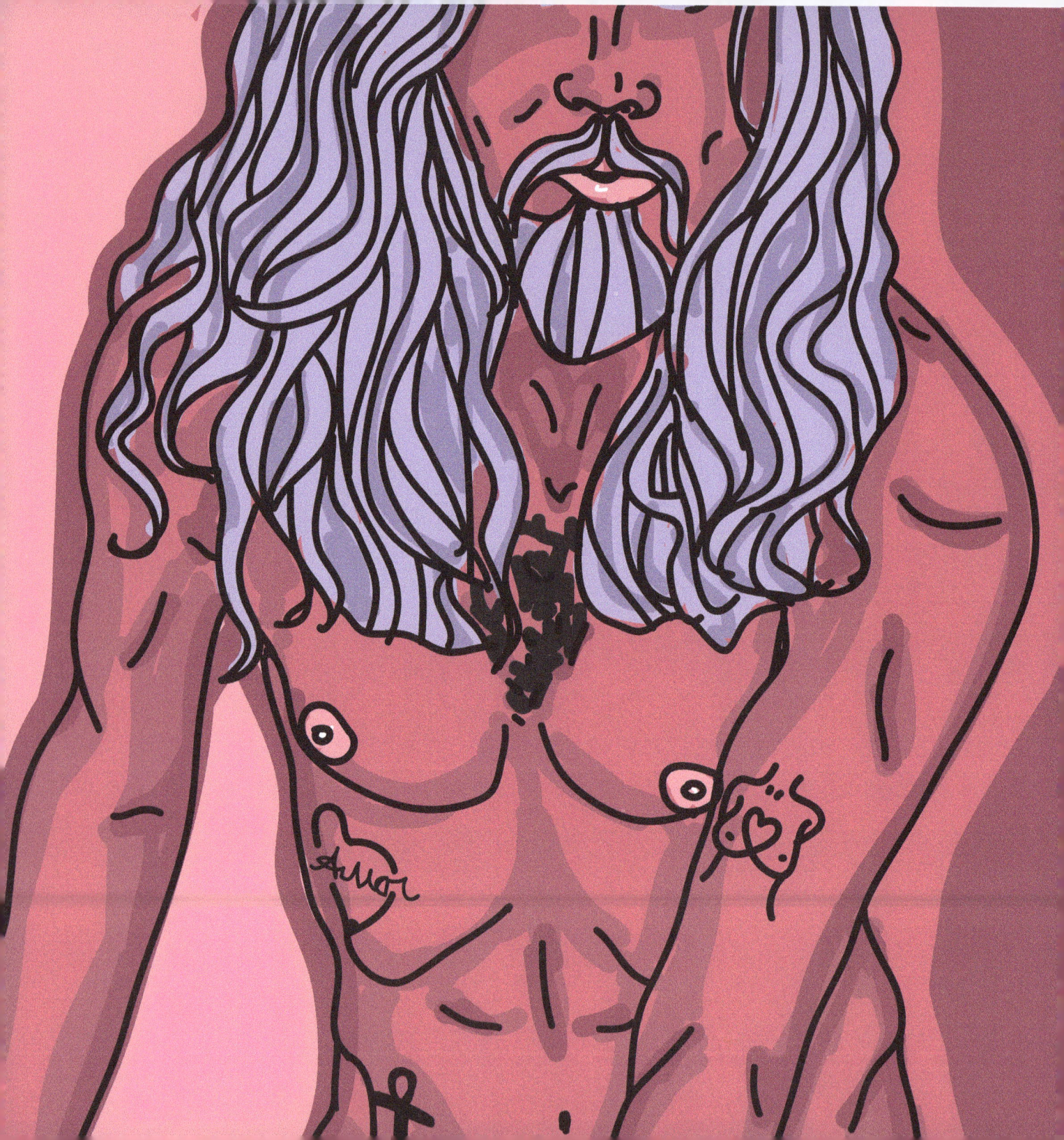

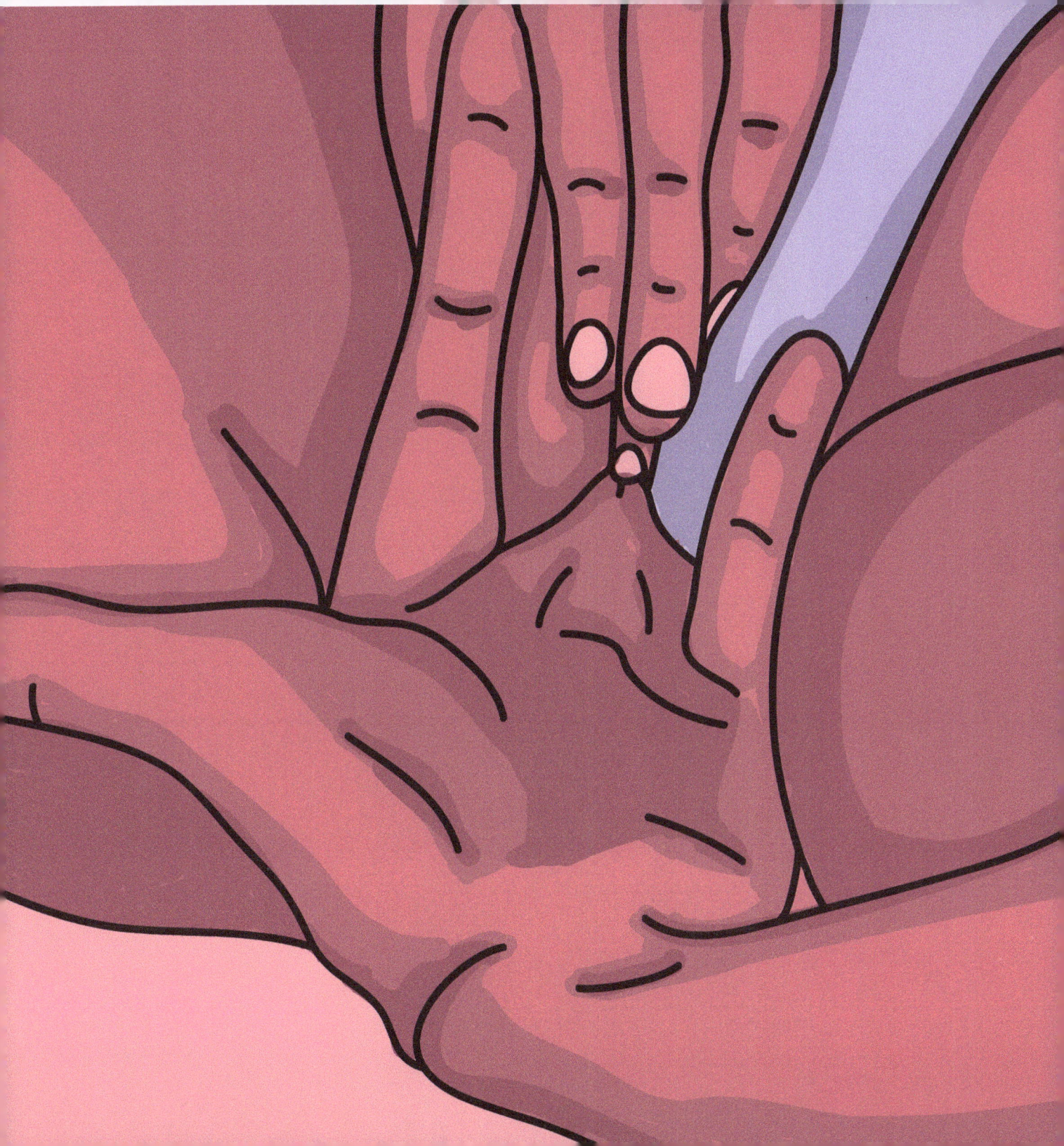

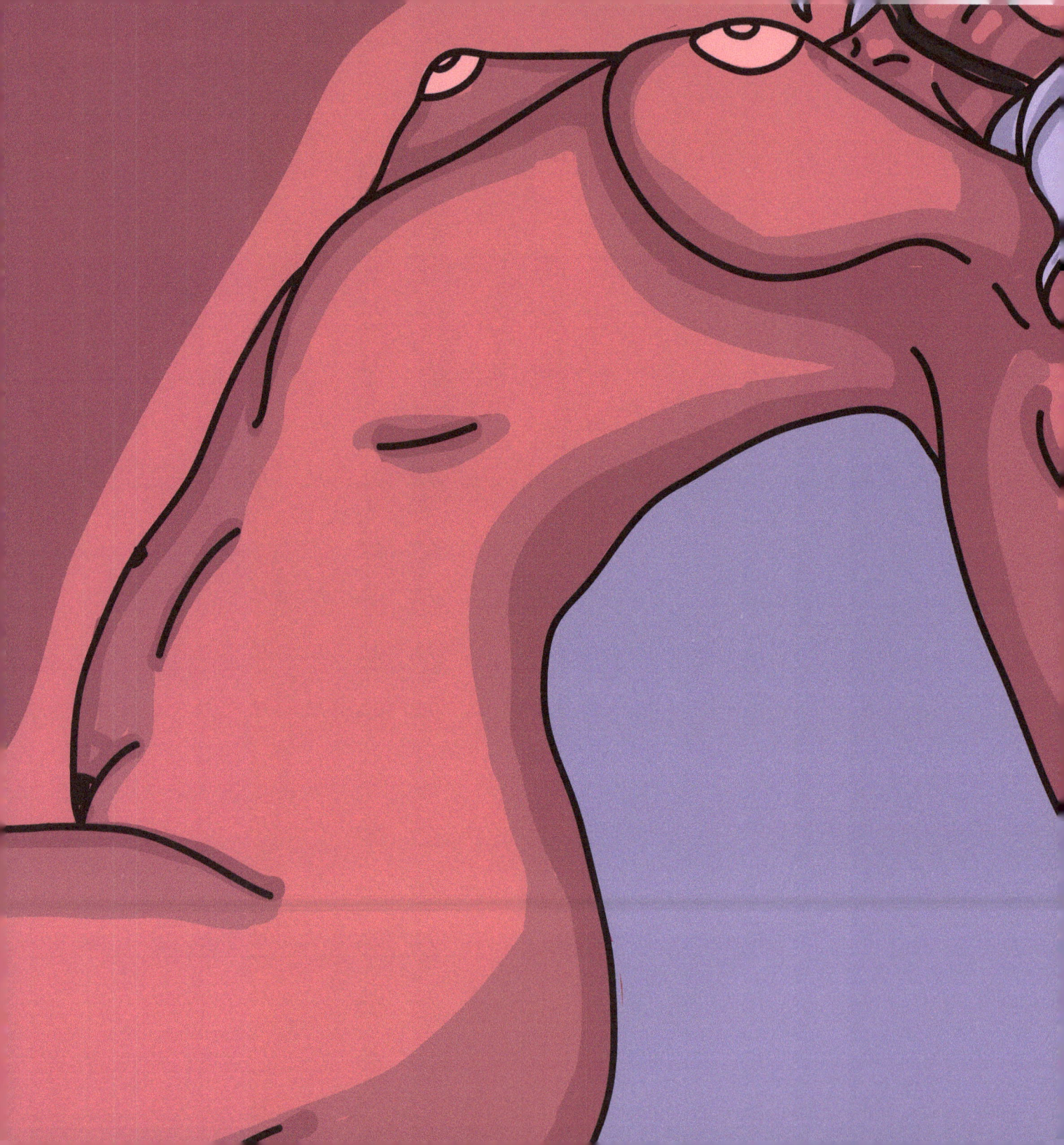

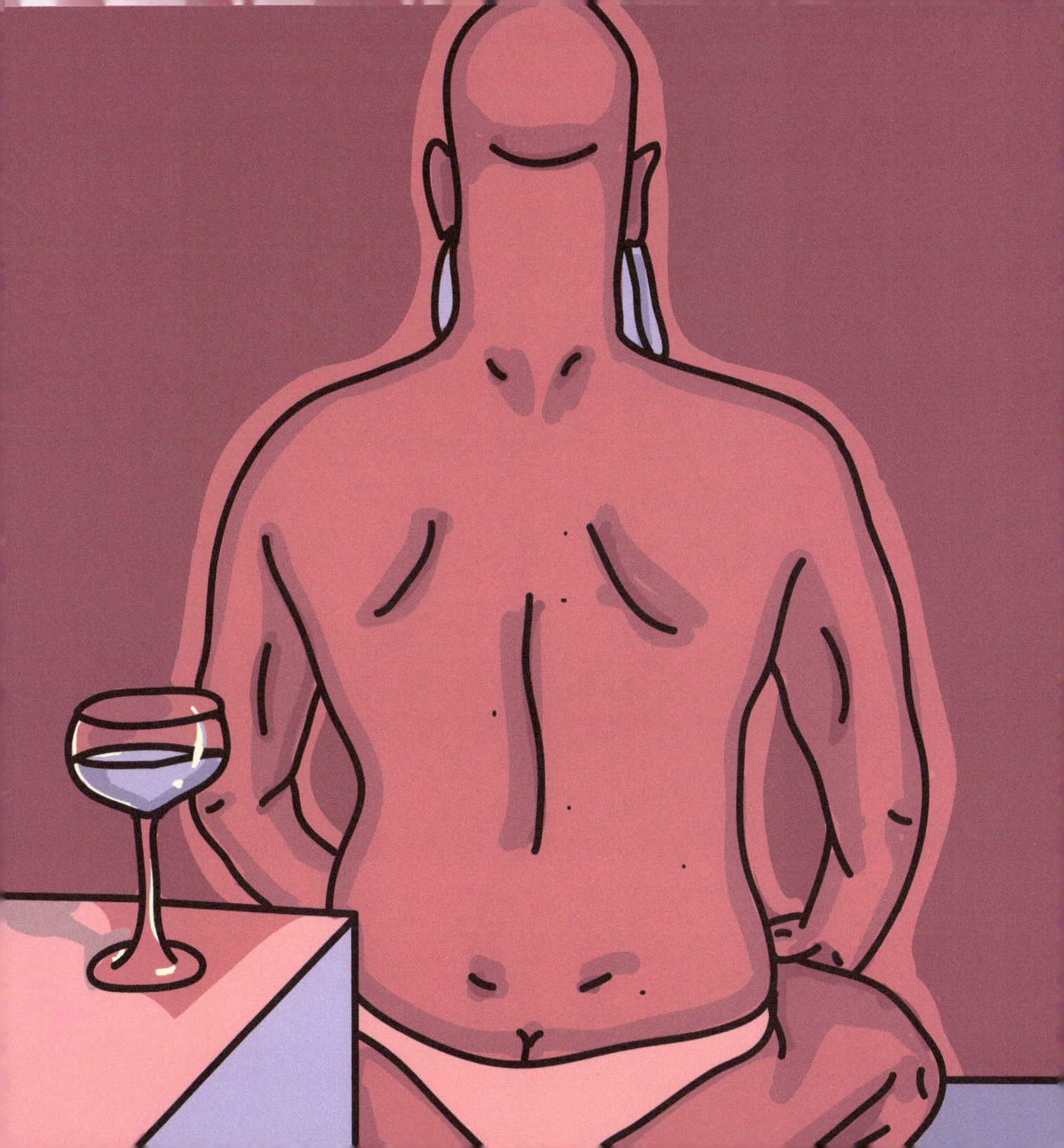

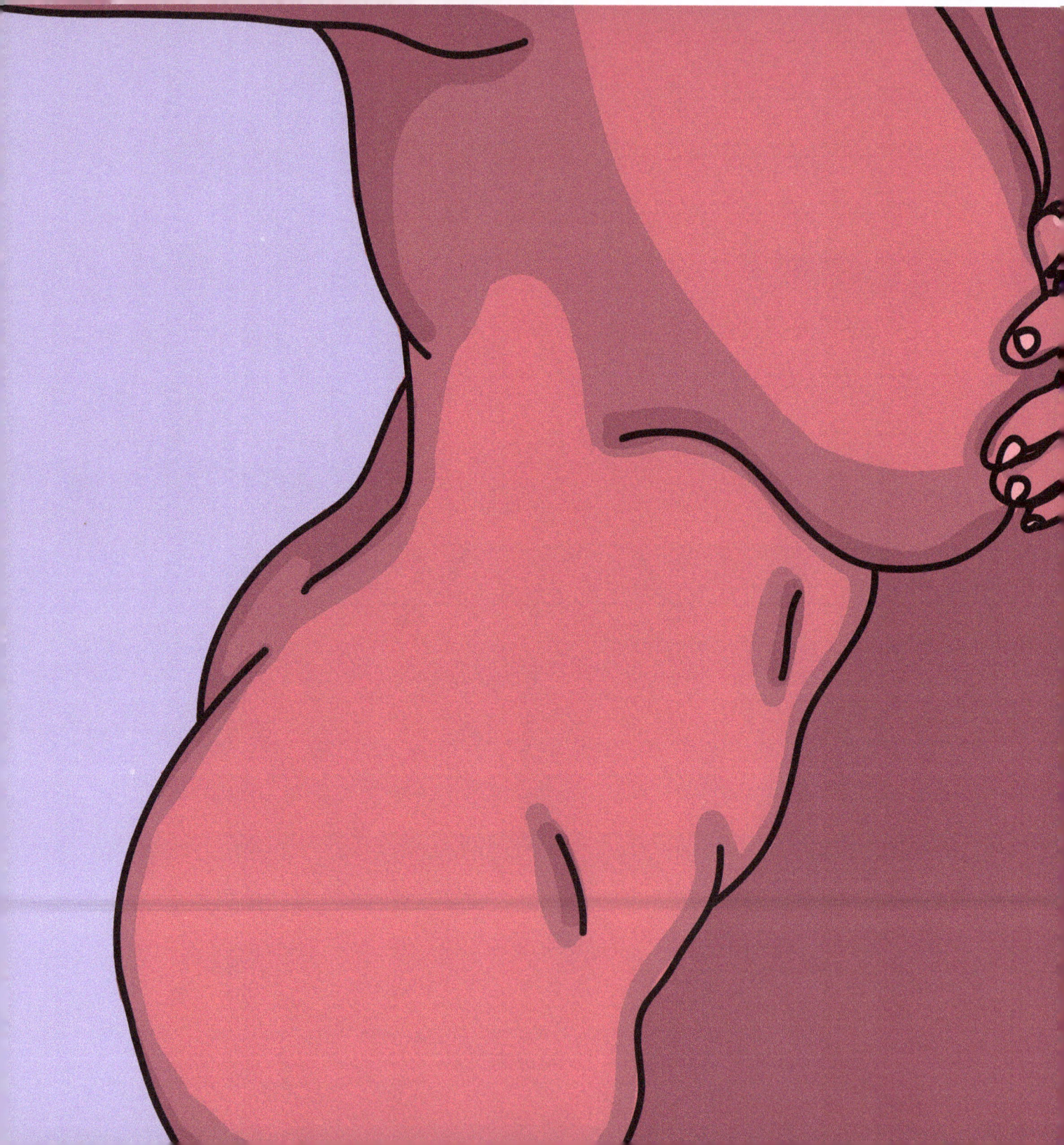

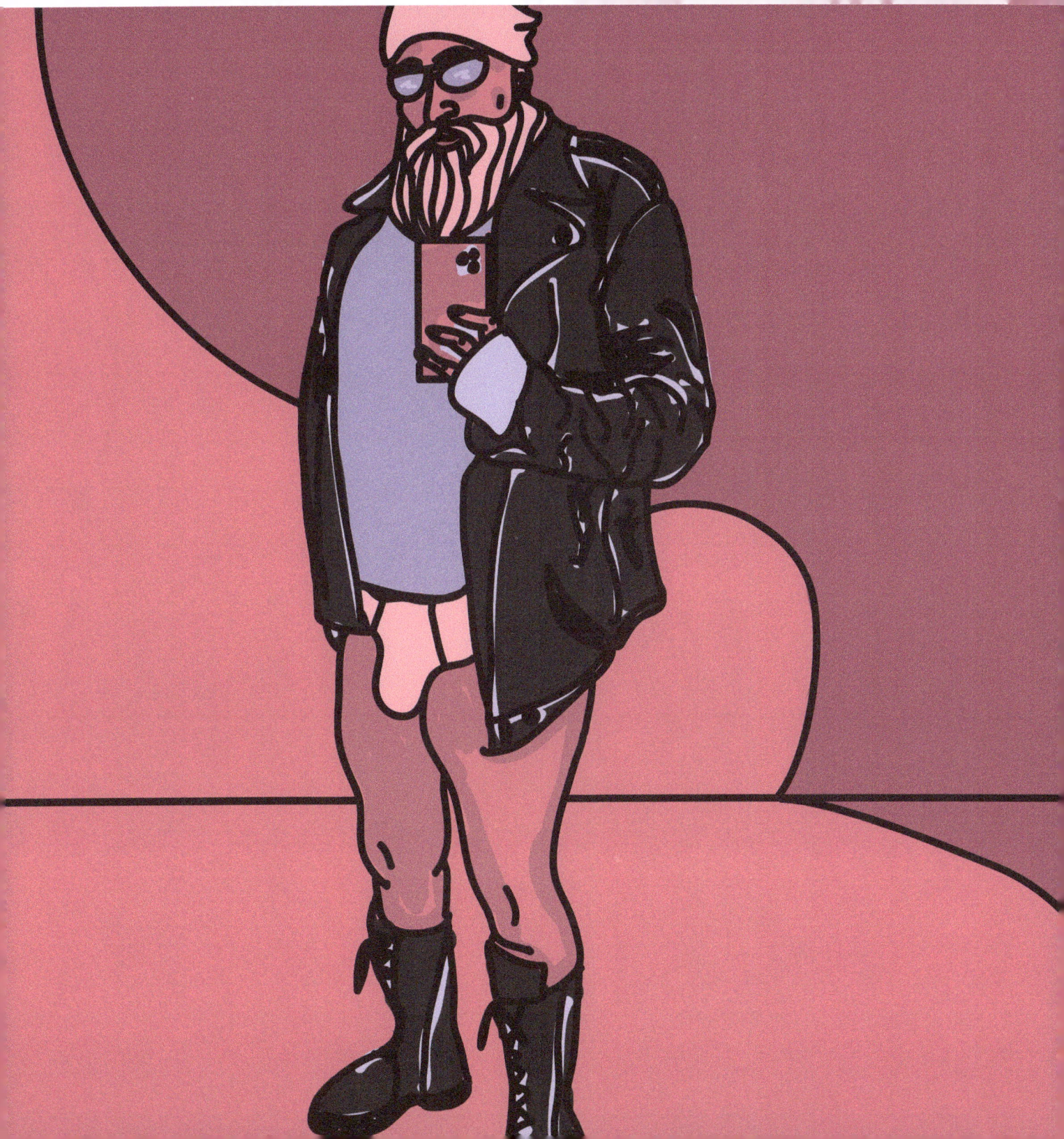

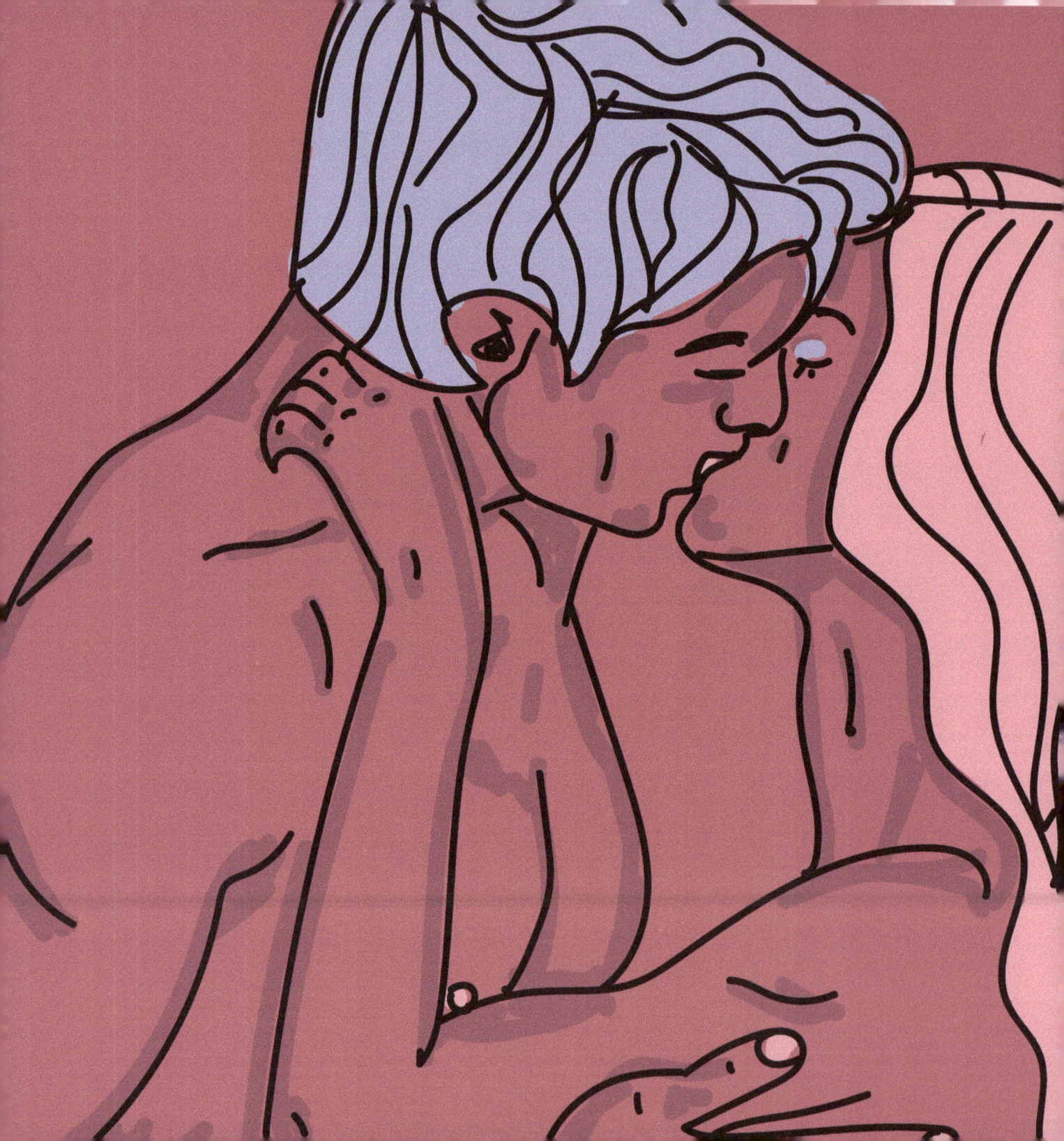

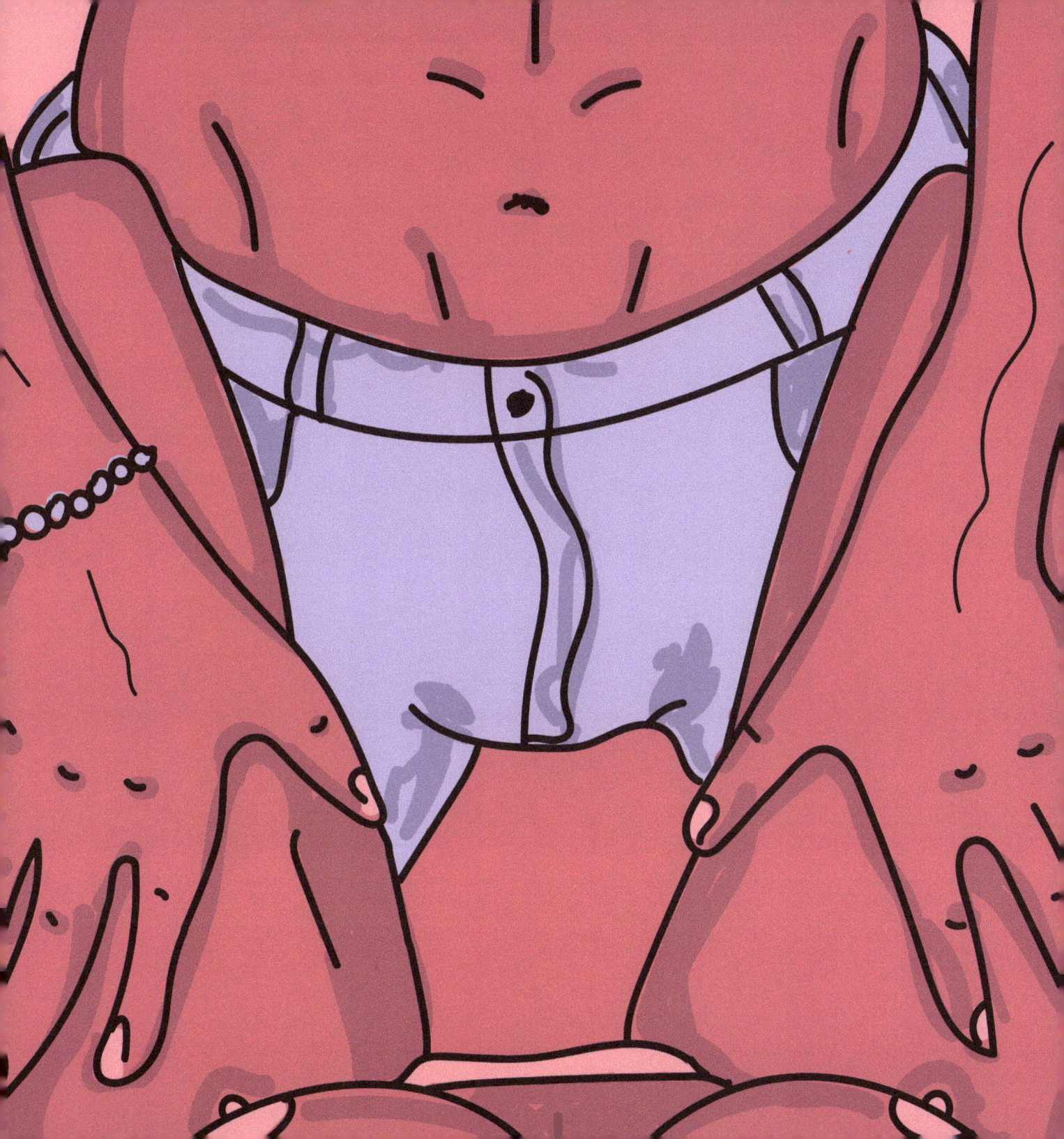

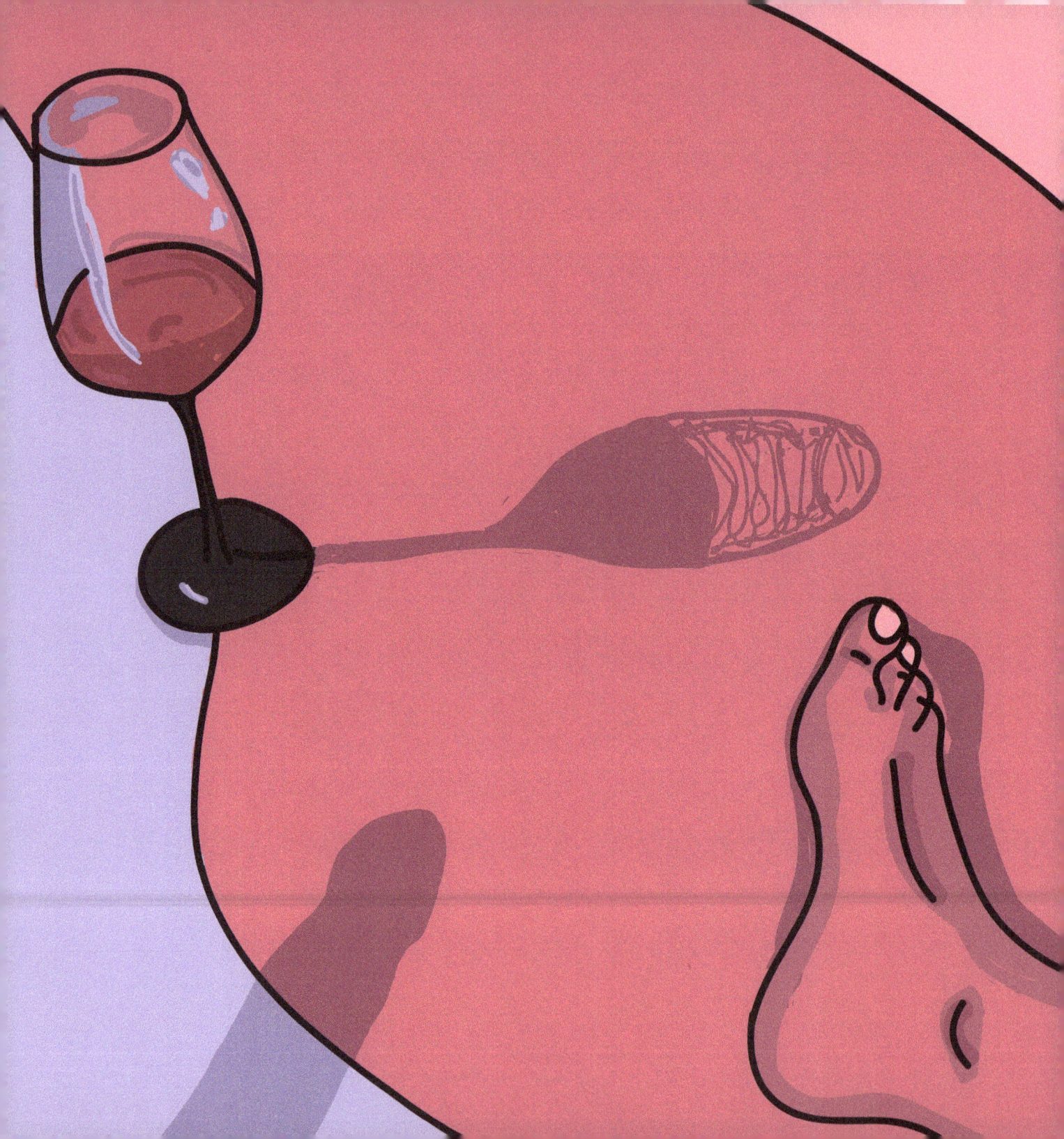

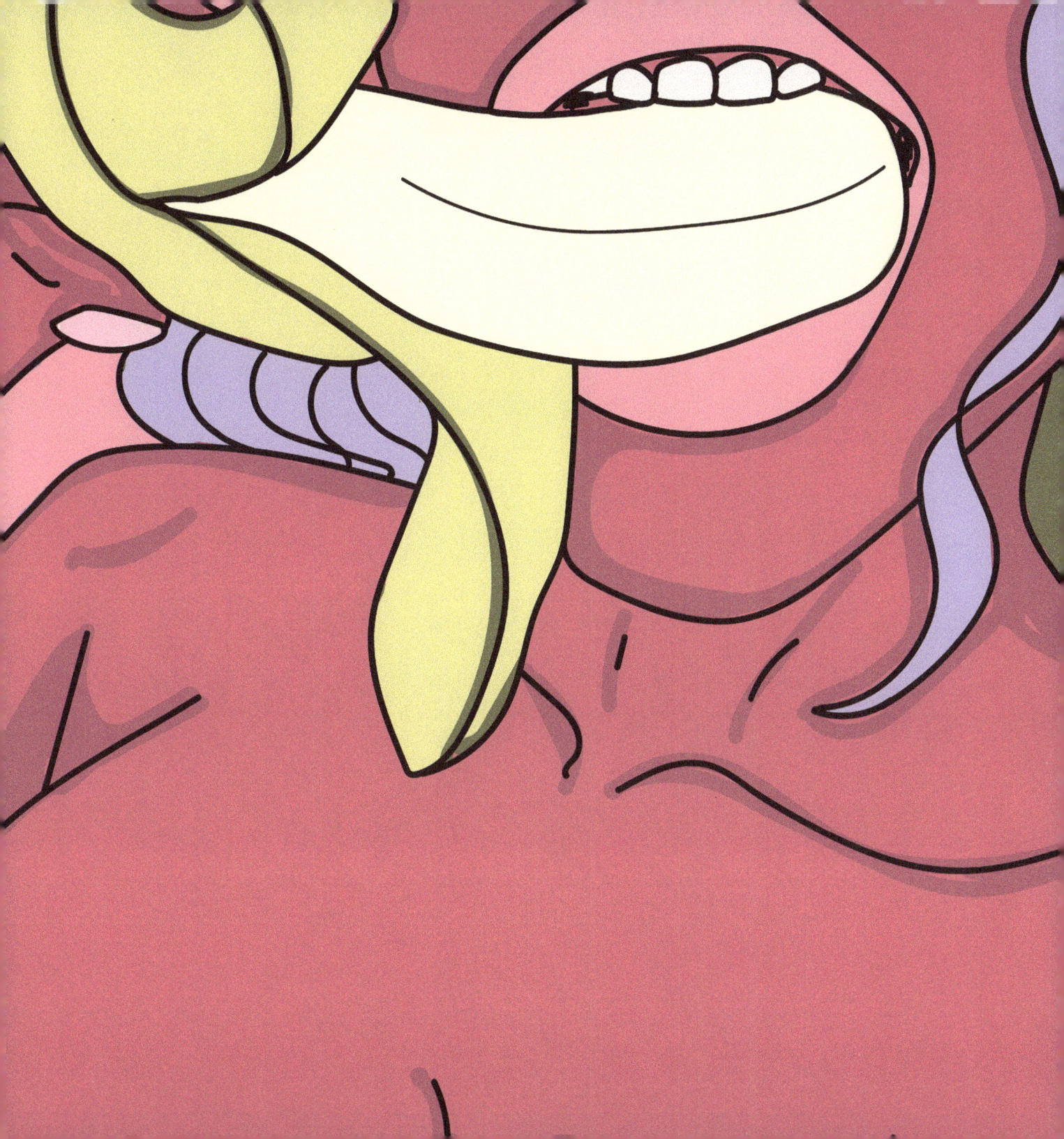

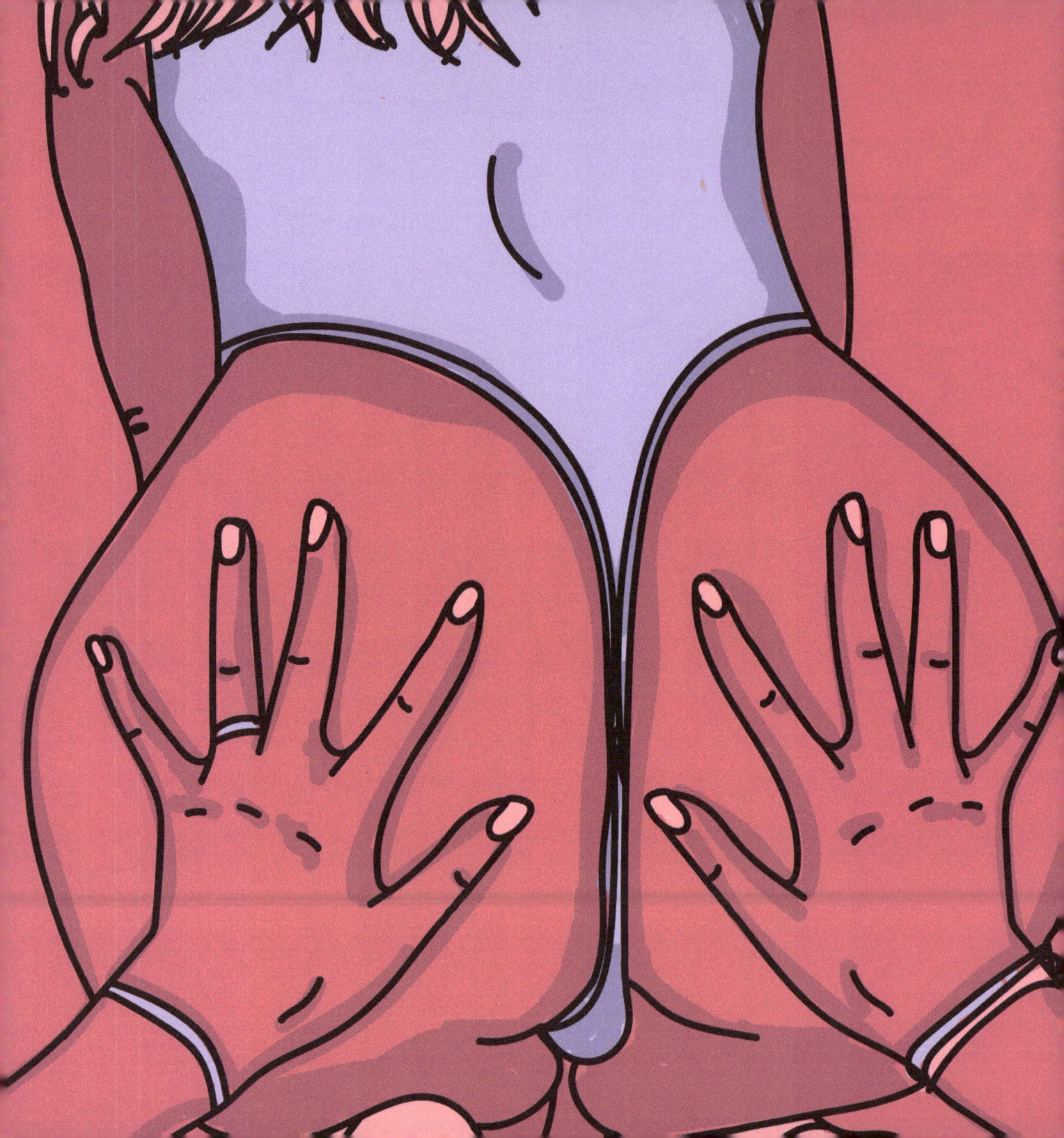

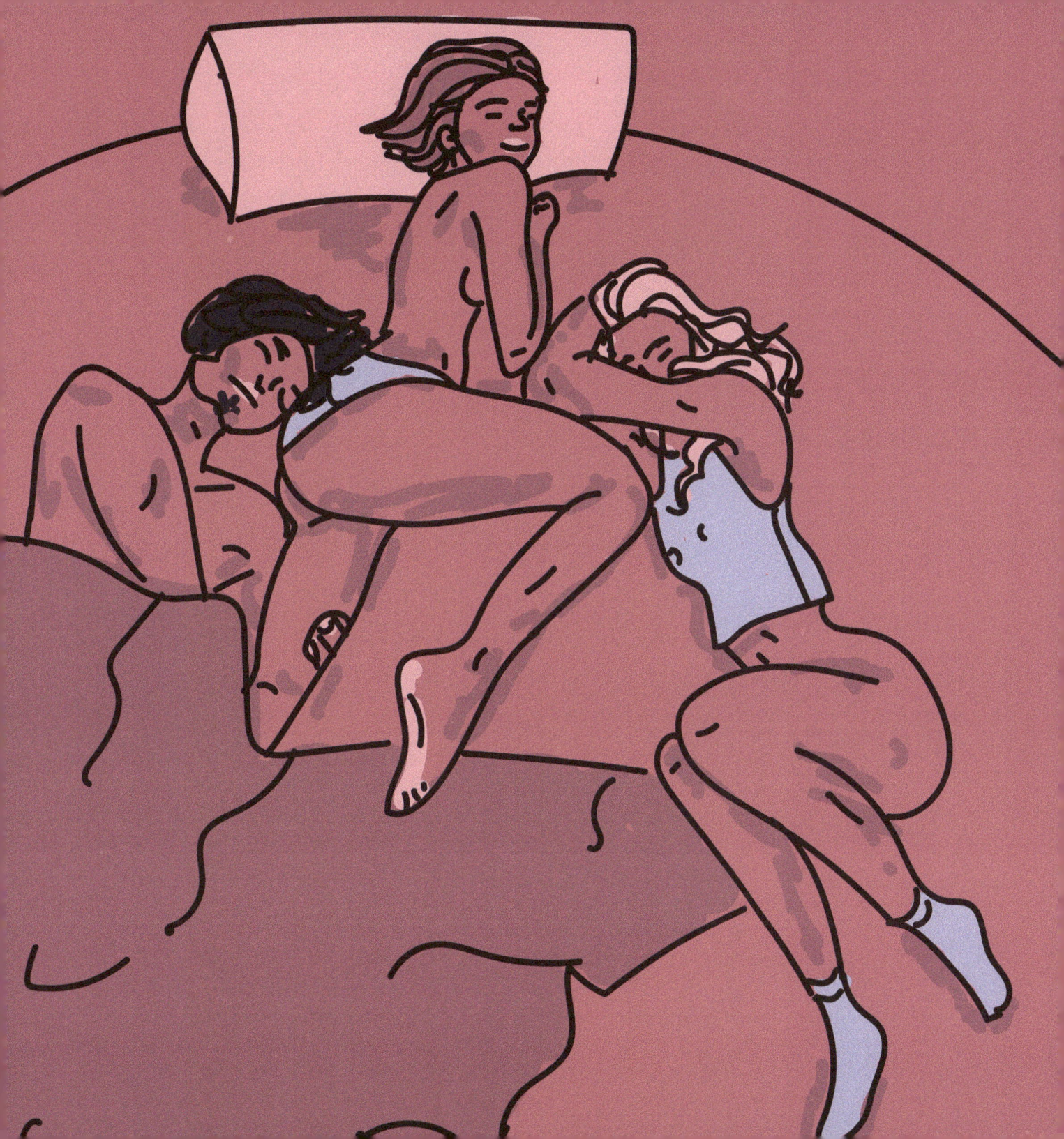

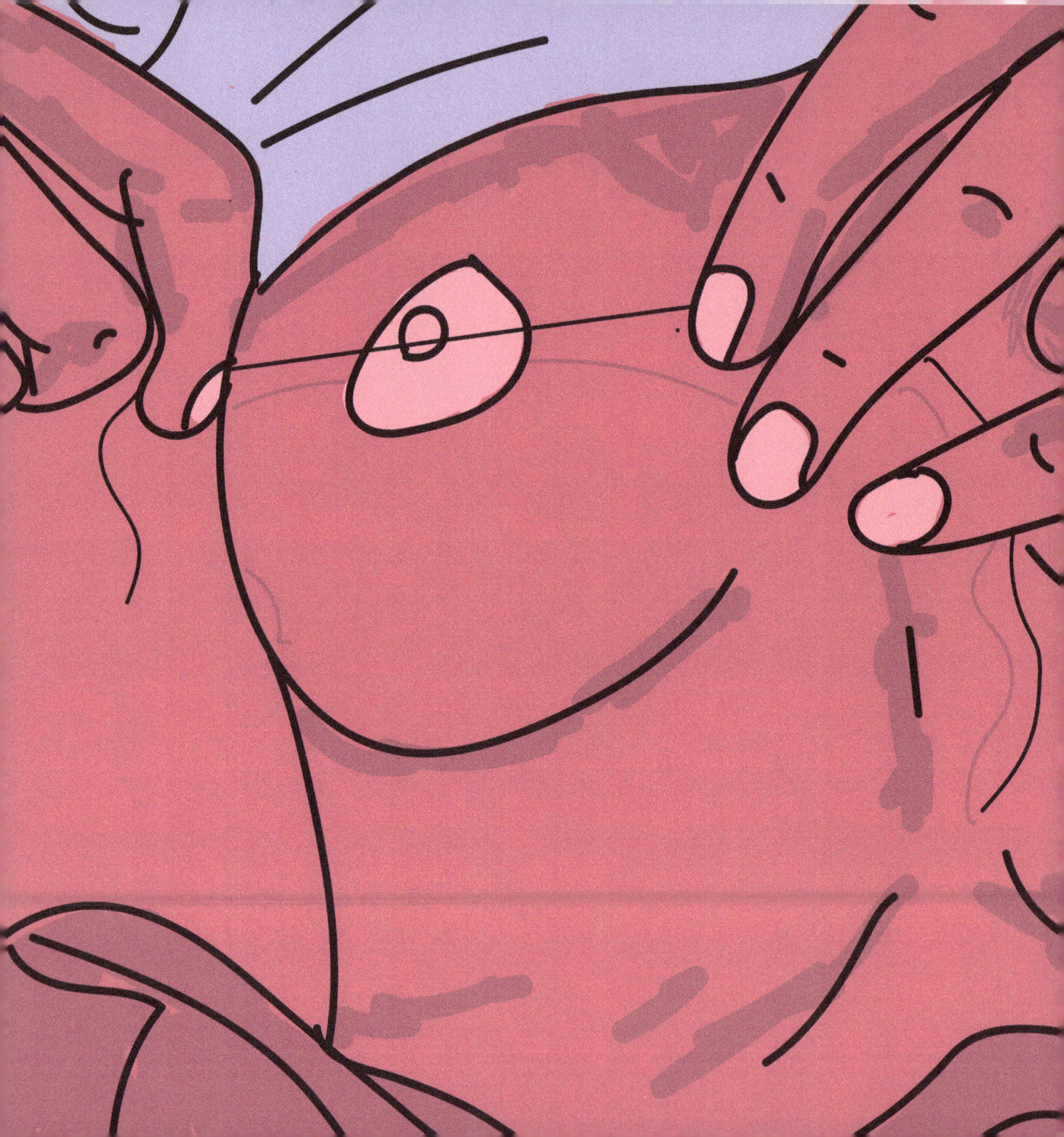

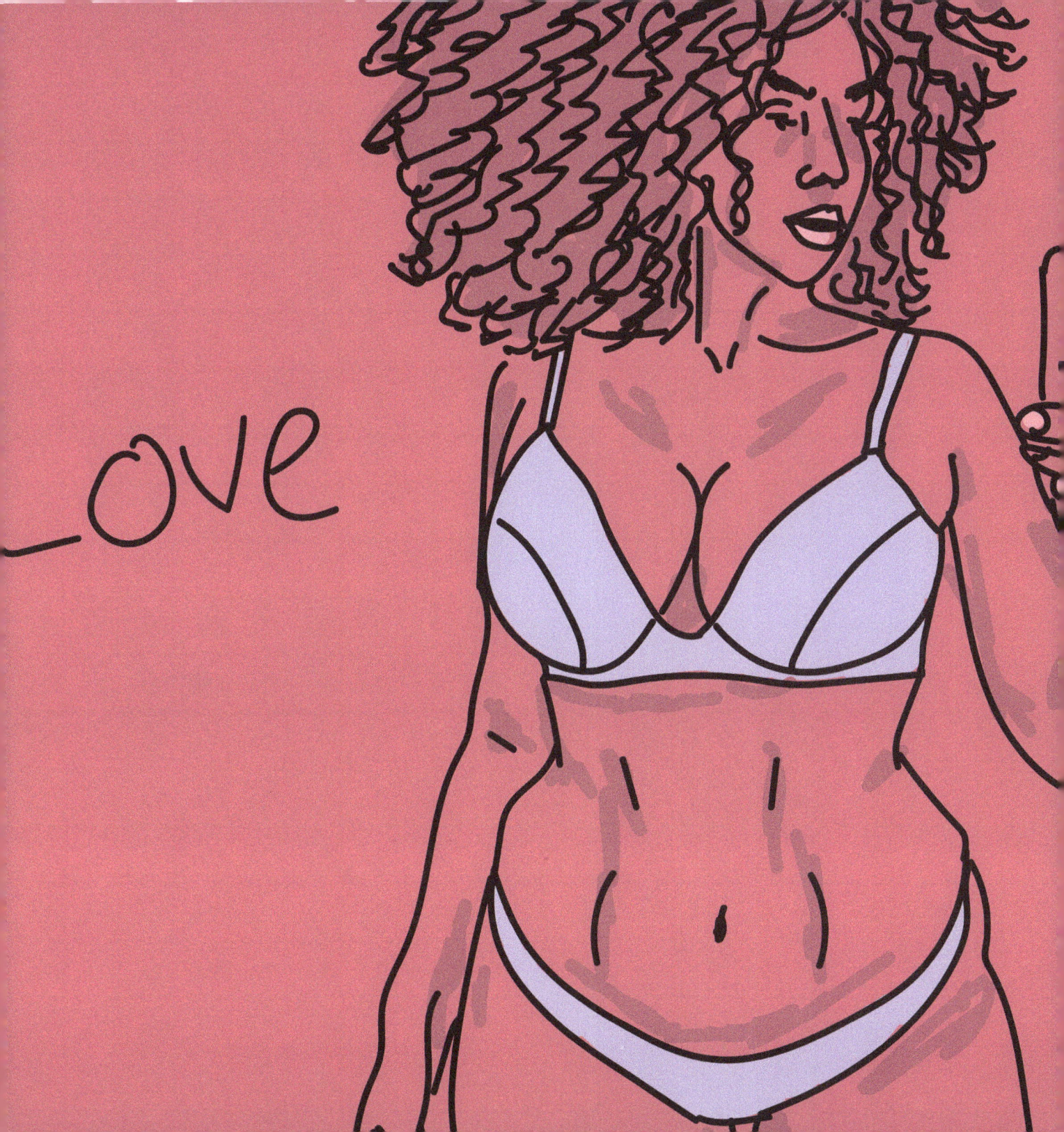

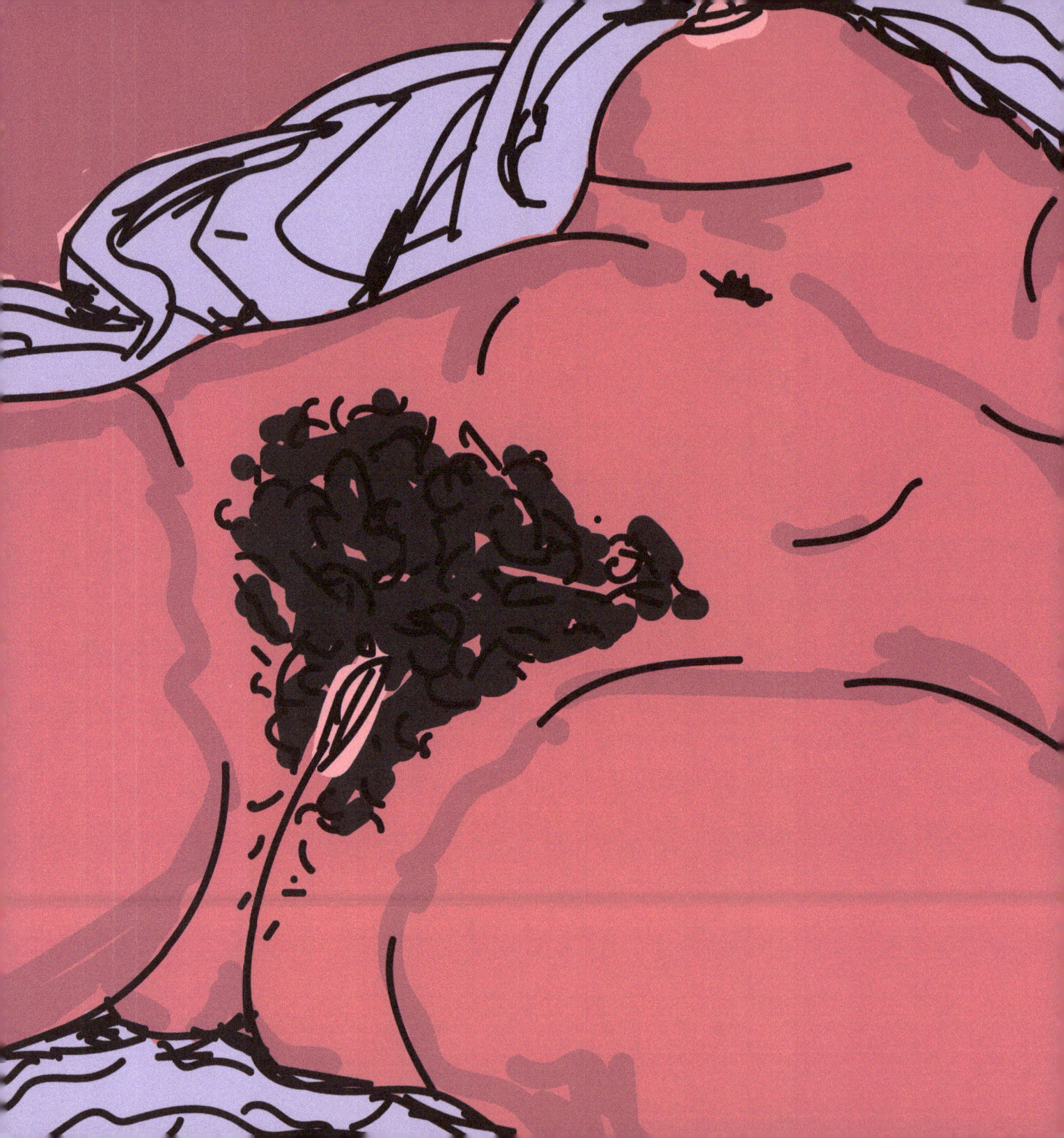

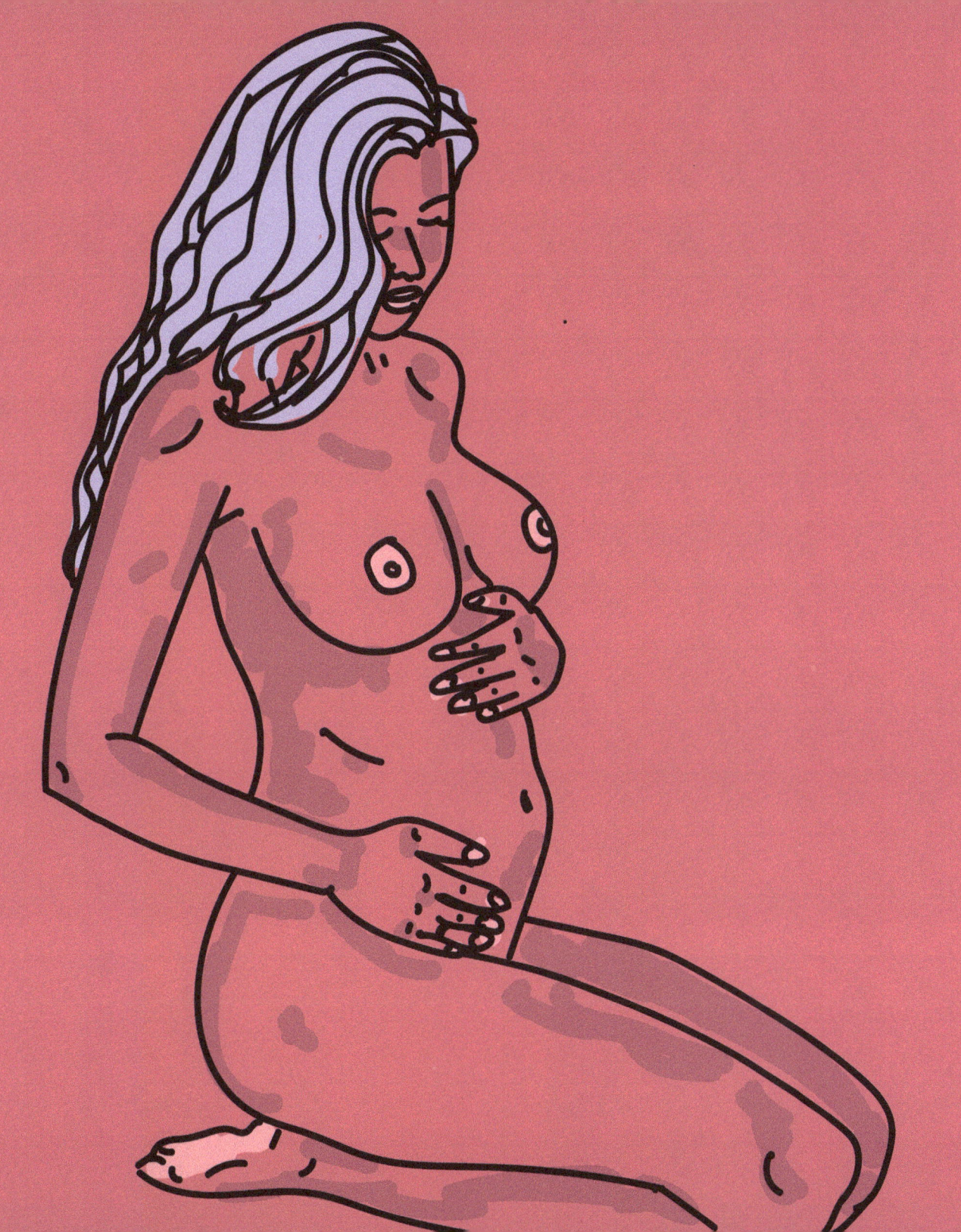

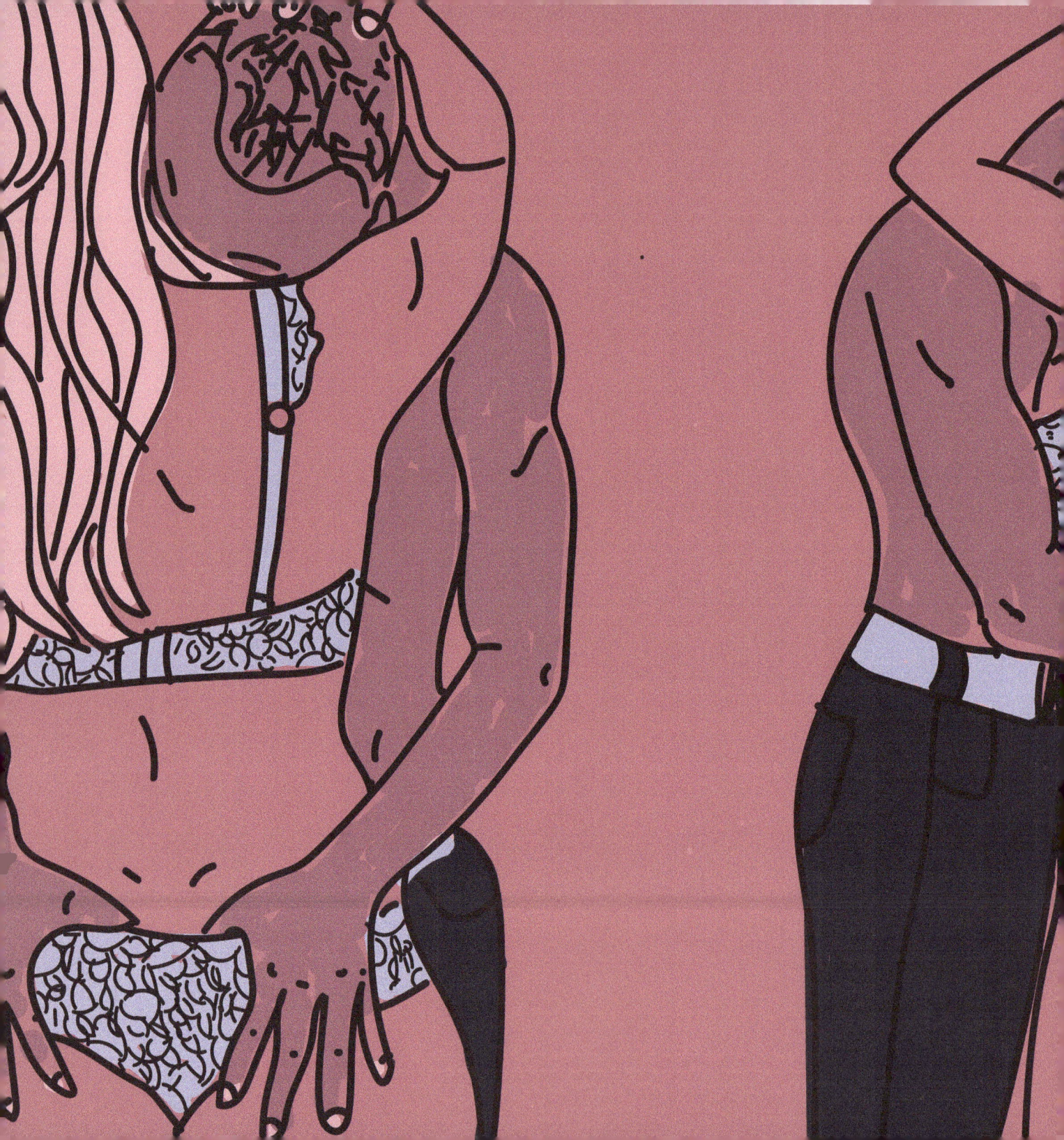

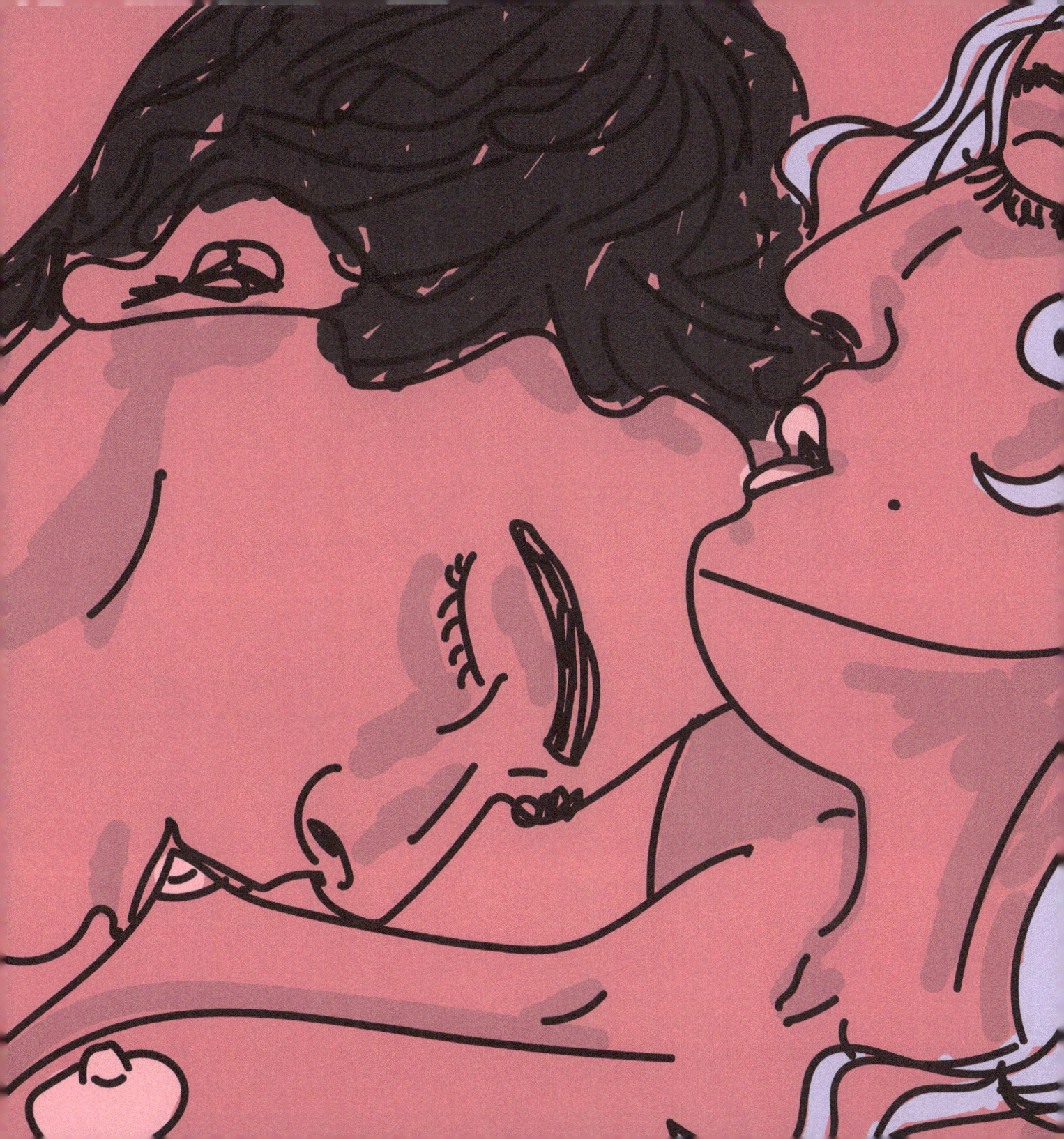

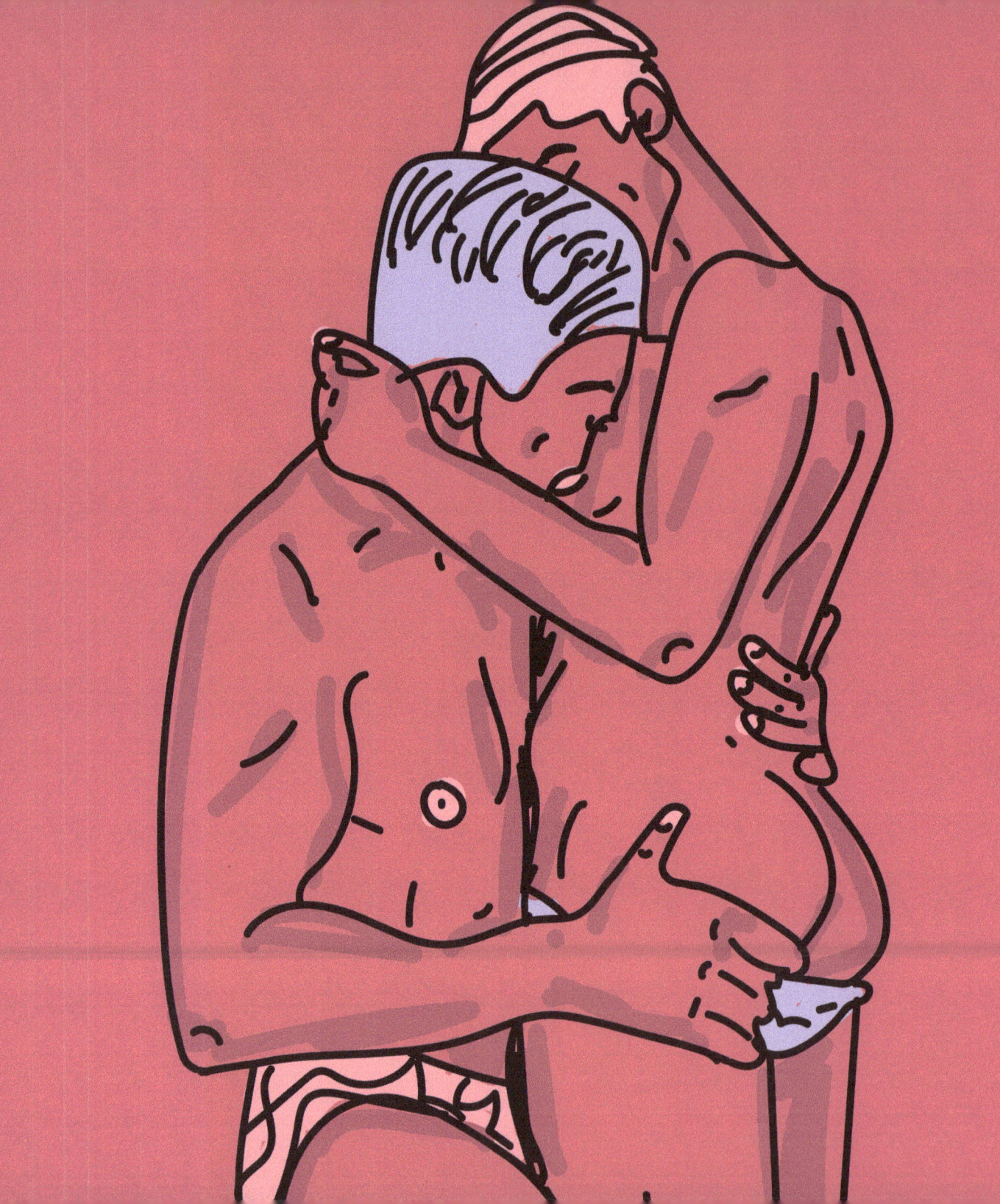

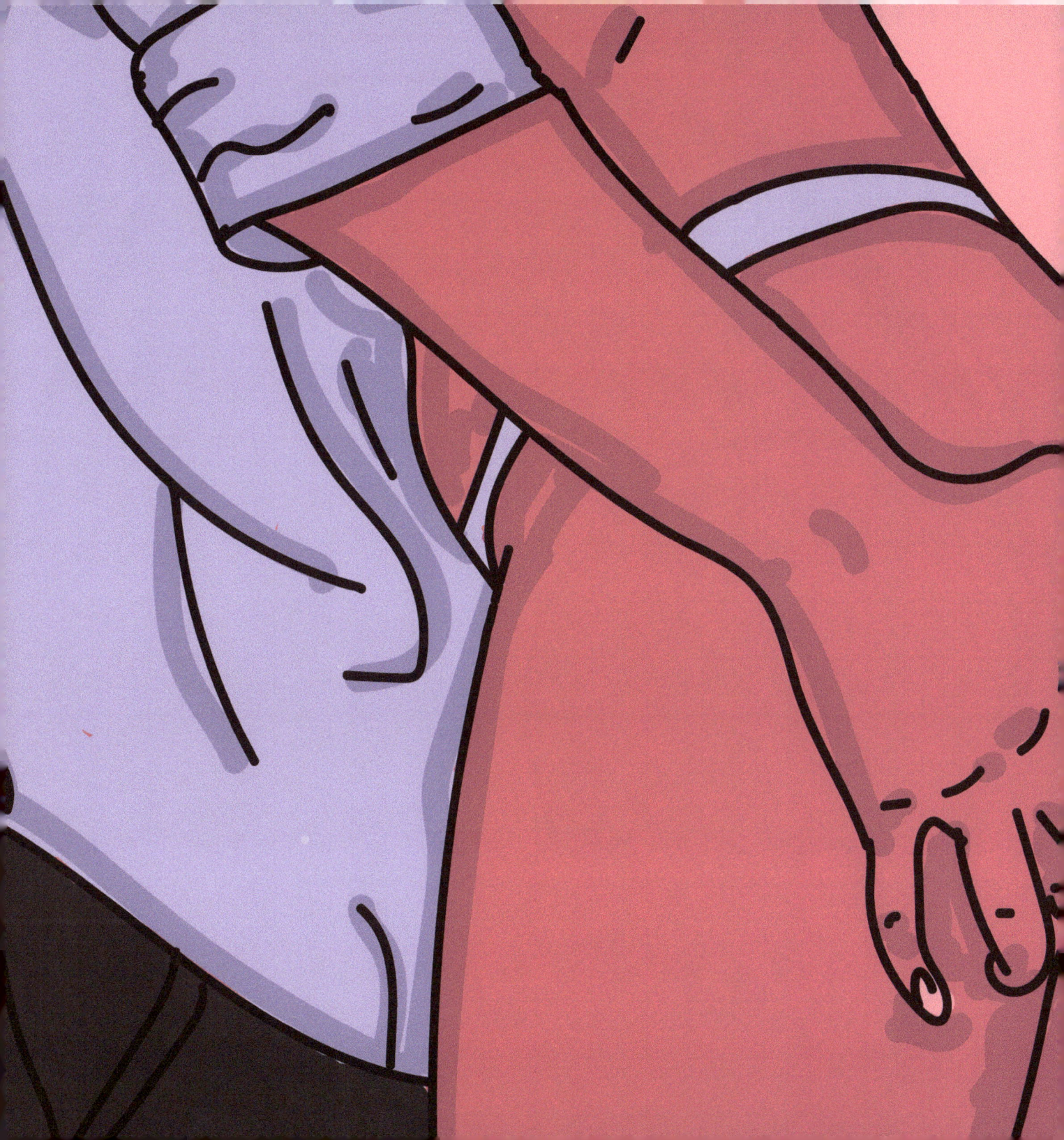

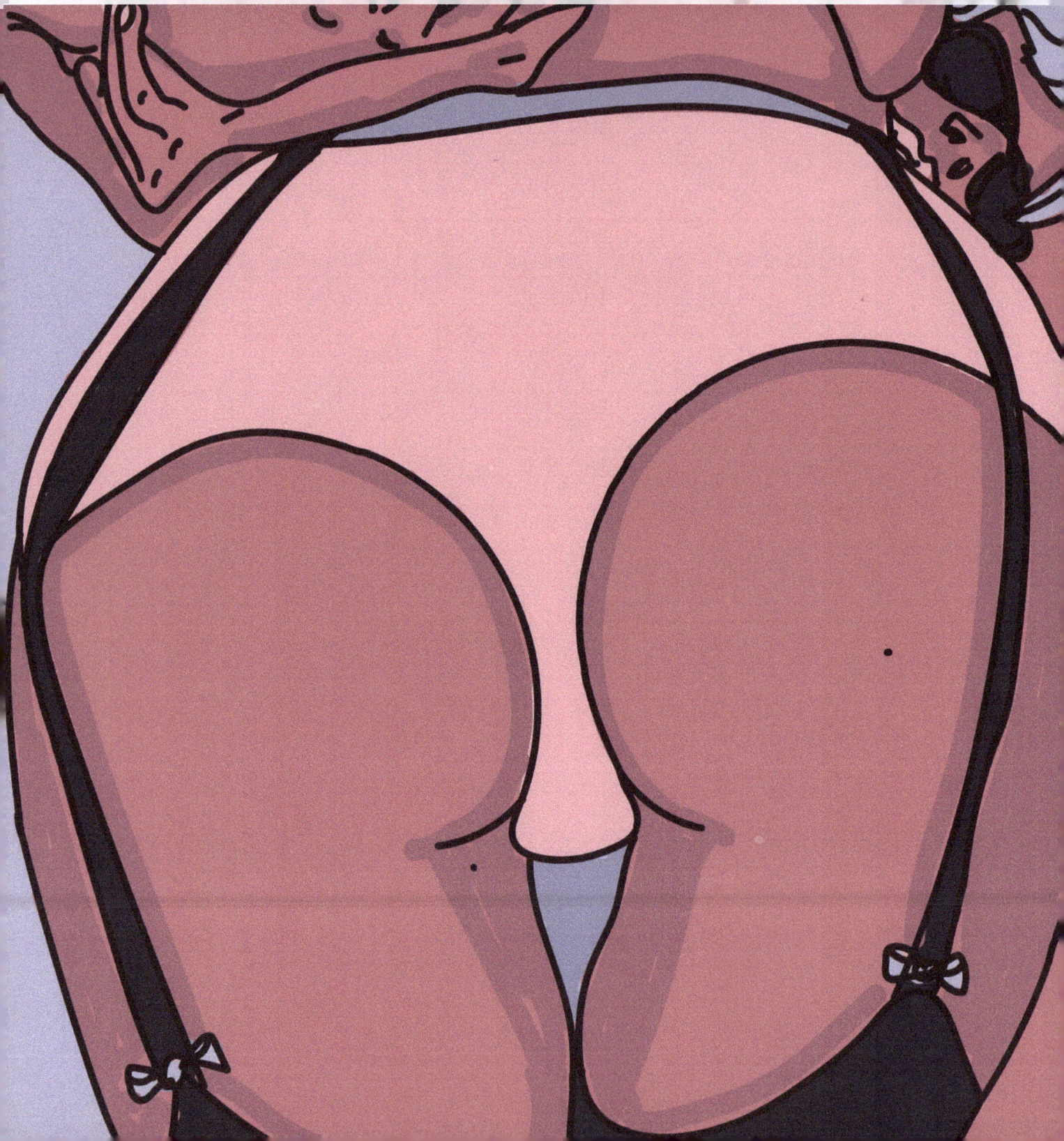

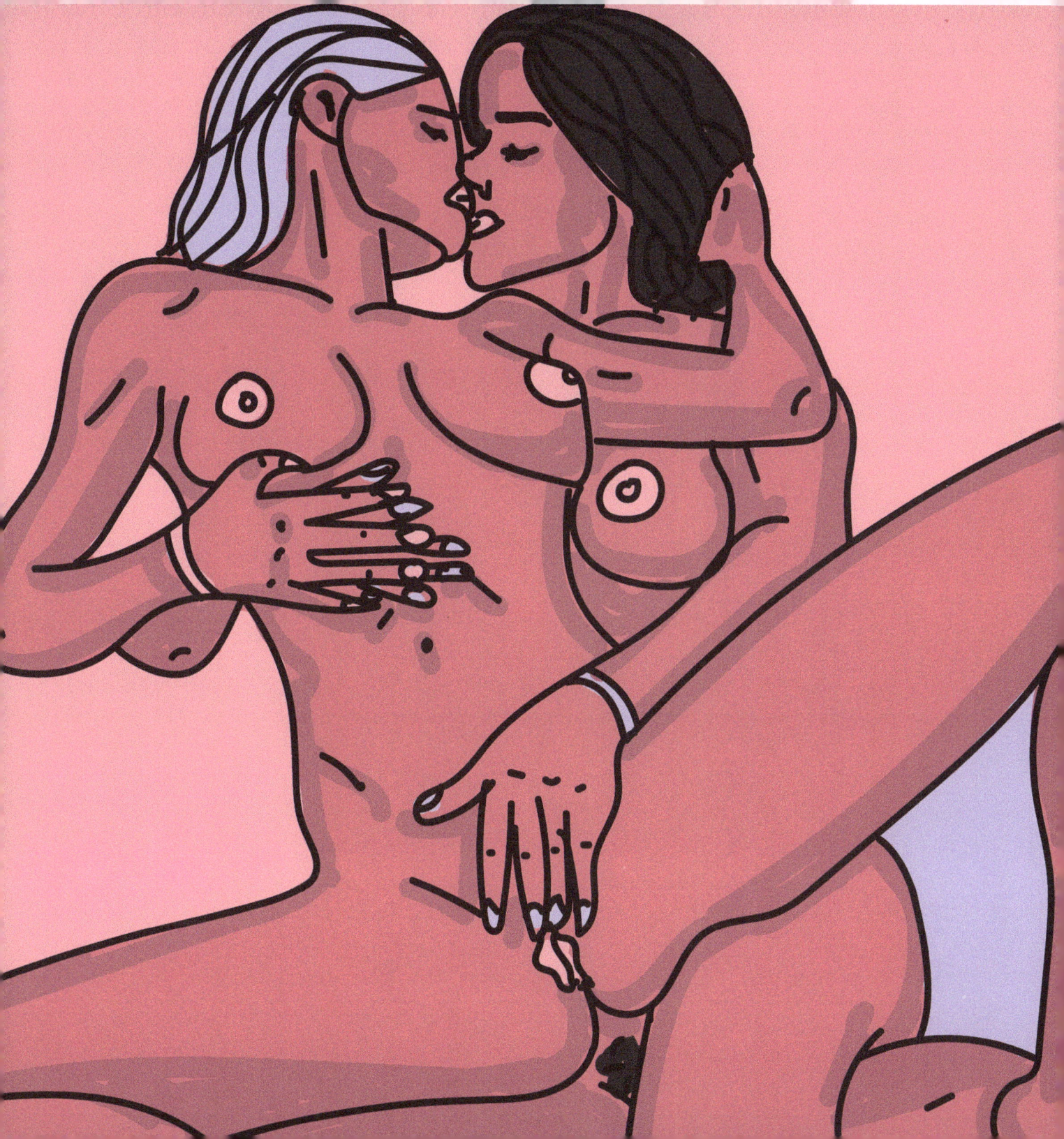

Peace Dream Love
(C) MMXXIV ALINA PATSUYK,
VAGABOND PUBLISHING LLC, VAGA-
BOND LTD. ALL RIGHTS RESERVED.

NO PART OF THIS PUBLICATION MAY
BE REPRINTED OR RECREATED WITH-
OUT EXPRESS PERMISSION FROM THE
PUBLISHER.

VAGABOND LTD
PUBLISHER@VAGABOND.LTD
WWW.VAGABOND.LTD

www.ingramcontent.com/pod-product-compliance
Lightning Source LLC
Chambersburg PA
CBHW040548220526
45473CB00017B/3052